PRAISE FOR PO'

"In *Power to Remember*, Jerem[...] Scripture memory into our modern [...] practical advice and inspiring encouragement, this book provides the why, what, and how to turn the daunting task of memorizing verses into a lifestyle of engaging Scripture. This is more than a technique. It is a lived conviction shared with passion, ingenuity, and joy."

WALTER KIM
President, National Association of Evangelicals

"Jeremy Kluth is a Bible man. He brings just what we need to build faith and tear down fear. This book goes beyond recitation. It helps us remember that the God of the book is best known through the book of our God. It's amazing how Scripture memory arms us with the sword of the Spirit in the midst of any battle. I highly recommend this helpful tool."

ROY PATTERSON
Community Relations Director, Moody Bible Institute
Moody Radio Host of Music for Sunday and Urban Praise

"After more than 40 years of preaching and pastoral ministry, one of my greatest concerns for each passing generation has been a decline in biblical literacy. As Christian leaders, it should trouble us deeply when we consider that believers are progressively fading in both knowledge and understanding of the Scriptures. This is why I am hopeful for *Power to Remember*. For a new generation of Christians, Jeremy Kluth is a much-needed voice. In *Power to Remember*, Jeremy offers a simple, practical, and powerful system for engaging and remembering Scripture. He also helps the reader to overcome typical challenges in memorizing and studying the Bible. I am confident that this book will help people of all ages and backgrounds to know and grow God's Word in their hearts."

REV. JAMES T. MEEKS
Founder and Pastor Emeritus, Salem Baptist Church of Chicago

"Jeremy Kluth makes a compelling case for the transformational power of Scripture memorization in his new book, *Power to Remember*. He guides you through a process that as you get into God's Word, it will get into you. Jeremy is on target to awaken this spiritual discipline in you and for generations to come. If you have not experienced the power of knowing God's Word in this way, then this book is a must for you. Don't miss how this practice will change your life, *forever*."

TAMI HEIM
President and CEO, Christian Leadership Alliance

"At Compass-Finances God's Way, we recognize that Scripture memory is vital to the life of every follower of Christ. Jeremy Kluth's Scripture Alive ministry and new *Power to Remember* book encourages and equips Christians of all ages to memorize God's Word and live a life pleasing to the Lord."

HOWARD DAYTON
Founder, Compass-Finances God's Way

"The study of Scripture, and especially memorization, provides a primary path to a deeper and more profound relationship with the Lord and others. I recommend Jeremy Kluth's *Power to Remember* book to Christians across the world to help them get deeper into God's Word and grow spiritually."

DR. STAN E. DEKOVEN
President, Vision International University

"The Scripture memory work I did has been foundational to every aspect of my life for the last 45 years; whether business leadership, interpersonal relationships, ministry work, family life, and my relationship with God. Jeremy Kluth has similarly invested in committing the Word of God to memory, and I have seen how transformative it has been in his life over these last two decades. This book is the fruit of his passion and investment in the Scriptures, and I highly recommend it for your own encouragement and transformation."

PETER MAYBERRY
Global VP for Leader Development, Awana Clubs International

"In *Power to Remember*, Jeremy Kluth has unlocked the secrets to releasing the power of God's Word into our daily lives. By using the simple strategies in this book the obstacles to "hiding God's Word in our hearts" can be overcome, giving the foundation and courage to live a fruitful life as God intended. We look forward to using this book wherever we provide Scriptures around the world, especially in the more challenging countries for new believers."

JOHN L. PUDAITE
President and CEO, Bibles for the World

"Scripture memorization became a powerful tool of transformation beginning in my teen years. Yet, it appears to be an essentially lost discipline to a generation bombarded with information and over-connected to social media. In his book *Power to Remember*, Jeremy Kluth provides a practical and compelling guide to begin the somewhat daunting task of renewing our mind through Scripture memory. Jeremy walks the reader through a simple plan and hands-on steps to begin the journey. If you are serious about renewing your mind through Scripture memory, this book is a great place to start."

DR. MARK JOBE
President, Moody Bible Institute
Senior and Founding Pastor, New Life Community Church

"When you hire a personal trainer or a business coach you look for someone who has experienced firsthand the success you're after. When it comes to memorizing Scripture, that's Jeremy Kluth! In *Power to Remember*, Jeremy lays out the path to successfully commit Scripture to memory. I applaud Jeremy for connecting memorizing the Word with doing the Word. Sometimes we miss this point and excuse either memorizing, doing, or both. *Power to Remember* is more than a book to be read. It is a pathway to be walked."

KEVIN WHITE
CEO, Spirit Media
International Bestselling Author and Speaker

POWER to *REMEMBER*

SCRIPTURE MEMORY THAT WORKS

DEUTERONOMY · EXODUS · JOSHUA
MATTHEW · MARK · LUKE · J
SAMUEL · 2 SAMUEL · KINGS · 2
...HIANS · 2 CORINTHIAN... · GALATIA...
...NICLES · EZRA · NEHEMIAH · ESTHER
...ETER · 2 THESSALONIANS · ...TIMOTHY
...ESIASTES · SONG OF SOLOM...N · ISAIAH
...ENTATIONS · EZEKIEL · DANIEL ...HABAKKU...
...ACTS · JOEL · AMOS · OBADIA ...ETER · ...
...KKUK · ZEPHANIAH · HAGGAI · ...ECHARIA
...HIANS · EPHESIANS · MALACH... · JONAH
...OSSIANS · 1 THESSALONIANS · ...THESSAL...
...OTHY · TITUS · PHILEMON · HE... ...WS · ...
...OHN · 2 JOHN · JUDE · ...EVELATION ·
...SAIAH · JEREMIAH · LE...TICUS · NUME...
...SALMS · PROVERBS · ...UDGES · JOH...
...OSEA · JOB · ROM... · OBADIAH · ...
...ES · 2 KINGS ...1 CHRONICL...
GENESIS · NA...UM · RUTH ·
· PHILIPPIANS ...COLOSSIANS

JEREMY KLUTH

FOUNDER OF SCRIPTURE ALIVE

Jeremy Kluth

Power to Remember

Scripture Memory That Works

By Jeremy Kluth

2023© by Jeremy Kluth

Printed in the United States of America

Spirit Media and our logos are trademarks of
Spirit Media

✨ SPIRIT MEDIA
www.spiritmedia.us
1249 Kildaire Farm Rd STE 112
Cary, NC 27511
1 (888) 800-3744

Books ›Christian Books & Bibles ›
Christian Living
Books › Christian Books & Bibles ›
Bible Study & Reference

Paperback ISBN: 978-1-958304-40-2
Hardback ISBN: 978-1-958304-39-6
Audiobook ISBN: 978-1-958304-42-6
eBook ISBN: 978-1-958304-41-9
Library of Congress Control Number:
2023900447

Register
This New Book

Benefits of Registering*

- FREE replacements of lost or damaged books
- FREE audiobook—*Get to the Point* by Kevin White
- FREE information about new titles and other freebies

spiritmedia.us/register

*See our website for requirements and limitations

I want to dedicate this book to my Lord and Savior, Jesus Christ. Through Him, I live and move and have my being. And without His Spirit dwelling in me, my desire to memorize Scripture and to stir up and instruct others to memorize Scripture would not exist. I am thankful for His living Word which He gave us, that we might grow in our knowledge, love, and understanding of Him.

Table of Contents

Acknowledgments

I want to acknowledge my dad for his unwavering love, support, and visionary mind. If you had not suggested that I launch a Bible memory and performance ministry, and teach others how to memorize Scripture, I might have never written this book. Thank you for always showing me that you want nothing but the best for me. I want to thank my mom, who is waiting in heaven, for showing me how to live like Christ. I want to thank my step-mom, Mary Ellen, for demonstrating what it means to have a welcoming spirit and a servant's heart. Thank you, Matthew, for introducing me to the medium of Scripture performance (i.e. Oral Interpretation) and being a great professor, mentor, and friend. I'm grateful to the many Bible performers and memory experts who've shared their wisdom with me, especially Aaron House of Piercing Word. I want to thank my editor, Carlene, for helping me see things that I couldn't see and making this a better and more holistic book that can reach and impact more people. As you like to say, "You can't know what no one has taught you." I also want to thank Kevin and his whole team at Spirit Media who championed this book and helped me in working out the title and subtitle of this book. I am better having worked with you. And most importantly, I acknowledge my Heavenly Father for His faithfulness and kindness. By Your grace, I am what I am.

Introduction

Our Power to Remember

Why is it so important for Christian believers to claim our Power to Remember?

To remember is so important to our faith that the verb appears more than 200 times in Scripture. Sometimes it describes how God remembers His commitment to His people. "I will *remember* my covenant between me and you and all living creatures of every kind," God tells Noah after the flood recedes (Gen. 9:15 NIV). Often it describes how God's people remember who God is and what He has done for us. In Deuteronomy, the Lord says through Moses, "You shall *remember* the whole way that the Lord your God has led you these forty years in the wilderness" (Deut. 8:2). God does not want His people to forget Him as their Lord and their God, nor to forget all that He did in saving them from the hands of the Egyptians. And just one verse later, we see God's desire for us to know that "man does not live by bread alone, but man lives by every word that comes from the mouth of the Lord" (Deut. 8:3). We are called to remember not just who God is and what He has done, but every word He has spoken, so that we may live by His Word.

When Jesus was risen from the dead and the women were looking for him in his tomb, two angels appeared before them and said, "...Why do you seek the living among the dead? He is not here, but has risen. *Remember* how he told you, while he was still in Galilee, that the Son of Man must be delivered into the hands of sinful men and be crucified and on the third day rise?" And they *remembered* his words" (Luke 24:5-8).

And importantly, our remembering guides our action. We don't just recall every word that comes from God's mouth, we live by them. We remember Jesus' death and resurrection when we take communion, as the apostle Paul tells us: "For I received from the Lord what I also delivered to you, that the Lord Jesus on the night when he was betrayed took bread, and when he had given thanks, he broke it, and said, 'This is my body which is for you. Do this in *remembrance* of me'" (1 Corinthians 11:23-24). He then clarifies the second action our communion includes: when we eat the bread and drink the cup, we proclaim the Lord's death until he comes (1 Corinthians 11:26). We are called to remember, and what we remember guides our action.

Power. It's a commanding word. It carries authority and weight. It can often have a negative connotation and many people use their power for ungodly purposes. But power, in regards to godliness, is one of the most extraordinary blessings God gives us. Directly before Jesus ascended into heaven, He had one final encounter with his disciples. When they all had come together, they asked him, "Lord, will you at this time restore the kingdom to Israel?" He said to them, "It is not for you to know times or seasons that the Father has fixed by his own authority. But you will receive *power* when the Holy Spirit has come upon you, and you will be my witnesses in Jerusalem and in all Judea and Samaria, and to the ends of the earth" (Acts 1:6-8).

The same power and Holy Spirit that were given to the disciples have been given to us, and it is the Spirit of God who raised Jesus from the dead (Romans 8:11). That is the resurrection power that was given to us. And since He lives in us, we have access to the Holy Spirit at all times, who also "brings into remembrance everything" He has taught us (John 14:26). And Paul tells us in 2 Timothy: "God gave us a spirit not of fear but of *power* and love and self-control" (2 Timothy 1:7).

This book is titled *Power to Remember* because these words are directly linked to what He tells us in His Word. The *power to remember* is central to our lives as believers. And that is the whole purpose of this book. I believe the content in this book and the POWER System contained within it will empower you to remember God's Word. It will empower you to overcome any excuses you believe about why you can't memorize Scripture.

God has given us the power to remember. We already have it. But the world, the flesh, and the devil have done everything they can to make us think we don't have that power. My prayer and hope is that my book is simply the vehicle for you to recognize and embrace the power that God has given you to remember His Word.

THE POWER TO REMEMBER IS CENTRAL TO OUR LIVES AS BELIEVERS.

Chapter 1

Reality Check

Imagine Life Without Your Bible

Digital marketer Joshua Summers hadn't lived very long in China before he ran afoul of local authorities and was arrested. Although he was in jail for less than a day, he quickly realized as the hours went on that all he had with him were his thoughts. He didn't have his phone or a book, much less a Bible. He started reaching down to find what he could recite from memory, and he realized how little he actually knew. And he decided to change that, which is when he set a goal to memorize the New Testament by the age of 40.

His time in jail was a reality check for him. He realized that without a text or a device, he didn't have access to God's Word. Because he couldn't muster much from memory, he was without the support, comfort and guidance that God intended him to have from the Word.

"When we have the entire Bible available as an app on our smartphones, it seems an unnecessary waste of time and effort to memorize specific verses or the grand narrative of the story," says Joe Carter of the Gospel Coalition. "By relying on technology to do our remembering for us, we have forgotten the moral aspect of memorization."[1]

Science writer Joshua Foer, who became a record-breaking memory champion, learned that in the ancient world "A trained memory wasn't just about gaining easy access to information, it was about strengthening one's personal ethics and becoming a more complete person."[2]

That is how the spiritual practice of Scripture memorization has improved Christian life and experience throughout the generations for many believers. When we invest in memorizing the Word, we allow the Word to wash over us and transform the renewal of our minds. I like to say that memorizing Scripture is never a waste of time; there will always be times when it's not possible to have your phone or Bible on hand. Some are relatively uncommon, like being imprisoned or living where the Bible has been banned. Others are more everyday scenarios, like where you're wrapped up in trying to calm your screaming child or meeting an urgent need at work. When you have His Word in your heart, the Holy Spirit will bring into mind just the right word, or phrase, or verse for you or for others.

In recent times, this ancient discipline has been cast to the wayside in exchange for letting technology do the remembering for us. Sometimes we even can make excuses for ourselves, like by pointing out that the Bible itself never uses the word "memorize."

It's true! Did you know that in the entire Old and New Testament there is not a single instance of the word "memorize"? Verses like Psalm 119:11 and Deuteronomy 11:18 use the words "hid" and "lay up," respectively, for this concept of someone memorizing or learning God's Word by heart, but there is no word that directly translates into the English word "memorize." That's partly because there is no Hebrew or Greek equivalent in the Bible, and that stems from the reality that the formal use of the word and concept of "memorize/memorization" is relatively modern. The word "memorize" was first used in the 1590s. At that time, it described the idea of keeping a memory alive so it wouldn't be forgotten, and included the idea of writing something down so the

WHEN WE INVEST IN MEMORIZING THE WORD, WE ALLOW THE WORD TO WASH OVER US AND TRANSFORM THE RENEWAL OF OUR MINDS.

idea couldn't be lost. It's not until the 1800s that we begin to see the word used to describe the idea of learning something by heart.[3]

It is true, of course, that the practice of memorization has existed throughout human history. Oral tradition has long been a way for people of all different cultures to pass down cultural practices and thoughts, stories, songs, and other forms of knowledge to the next generation. This was a very natural and effective way for people to "memorize" different things and it is still something you can find practiced today in all four corners of the earth in one form or another. But knowing these things from memory for much of the history of the oral tradition was out of necessity because passing things down by word of mouth came from the lack of having written literature to refer to.

Job, a godly man who lived in the time after the tower of Babel and sometime in the time of the patriarchs Abraham, Isaac, and Israel, says, "I have not departed from the commandment of his lips; I have treasured the words of his mouth *more* than my portion of food" (Job 23:12, emphasis added).

At this time Job would not have had any page of inspired writing and yet God talked to Him, and Spurgeon says, "That what God had spoken to him he treasured up. He says in the Hebrew that he had hid God's Word more than ever he had hidden his necessary food. They had to hide grain away in those days to guard it from wandering Arabs. Job had been more careful to store up God's Word than to store up his wheat and barley; more anxious to *preserve the memory* of what God has spoken than to garner his harvests" (emphasis mine).[4]

And if we jump ahead to the time of Moses, when God gives him the Ten Commandments, it says in Deuteronomy that "Moses summoned all Israel and said to them, "*Hear*, O Israel, the statutes and the rules that I speak in your *hearing today*, and you shall learn them and be careful to do them" (Deut. 5:1, emphasis added). He goes on to say in the next chapter in one of the most famous passages in the Old Testament, "*Hear*, O Israel: The Lord our God, the Lord is one. You shall love the Lord your God with all your heart and with all your soul and with all your might. And these words that I command you today shall *be on your heart*. You shall teach them diligently to your children, and shall talk of them when you sit in your house, and when you walk by the way, and when you lie down, and when you rise. You shall bind them as a sign on your hand, and they shall be as frontlets between your eyes" (Deut. 6:4-8, emphasis added).

The majority of the Israelites did not have the written Word to refer to for memorization, at least not the whole thing. For them, it was about *hearing* it and then responding in faith by doing it, which included having it in their heart, teaching it to their children, talking about it in the house and out and about – in essence – that God's Word would permeate their entire life. And that did include some writing as verse nine of Deuteronomy 6 says, "You shall *write them* on the doorposts of your house and on your gates." But even in that it was so they could see it each and every day to be reminded of God's Word and learn it by heart through that repetition, which most likely included reciting it out loud and sharing it with their children.

So the literal practice of memorization can be traced back to the beginning of human language and culture. Whether or not it stems from necessity as a result of the lack of written literature, people memorized because humans are forgetful. No wonder then that one of the most common commands in Scripture is to remember. Our Creator, the One in whose image we are made, knows how easy it is for us to forget Him, to forget His Word, and to forget what He's done for us. That's why He commands us often, through Himself, through a chosen leader, or through a messenger to remember His faithfulness, His good deeds, and His words (Deut. 8:2, 1 Chron. 16:12, Luke 24:6).

But remembering is not the same as memorizing. Remembering is the act of calling to mind something that we have *already* stored up in memory, and some of the things we remember get stored away without any conscious effort. We might recall the smell of a favorite dinner being cooked or our excitement when a toddler took her first step, and we know we didn't work to memorize those things. But if we remember our childhood street address, a friend's phone number, a Scripture verse, or a fact needed in our job, it's more likely we made the effort to commit those things to memory.

The reason the formal use of the word and concept of memorization are relatively modern is because newer technologies give us the luxury of not needing to remember very much. With the invention and development of the printing press in the 15th century, written culture began to overtake oral culture. As literacy improved and more things were written, the burden of needing to recall something that was said or heard was greatly reduced. As my grandpa liked to say, "A short pencil is better than a long memory."

Before written cultures and rising literacy rates emerged, the concept of memorization didn't exist because people didn't know any way to remember other than to learn things by heart. Memorizing was a daily part of life, so much so that there didn't need to be any phrase for it. I think of breathing and how it is so central to who we are that we don't think about it. We know subconsciously that we are doing it

ONE OF THE MOST COMMON COMMANDS IN SCRIPTURE IS TO REMEMBER

and it's because our bodies need oxygen but I don't think any of us, (outside of times of stress or other necessary situations), need to will ourselves to breathe. We don't need to say to our bodies, "Okay, you better breathe, body, because I am going to be in big trouble if you don't."

In the same way, putting things to memory is a daily part of life in an oral culture. It didn't require as much intentional thought as it does today. It took effort to be sure; that's why there are the commands to remember. People still forgot things in oral cultures, but people had greater capacity to remember more things with greater ease because memorization was ingrained in the fabric of daily life. Today, because of our ability to access content in print and online, and because we can create written and digital reminders for ourselves, our capacity to remember has decreased. We have lost the need for memorization, and we've lost the practice of subconsciously and consciously repeating large volumes of material that has been passed down through word of mouth.

"Our information age has accustomed us to retrieve massive amounts of information quickly and easily," observed Bob Banks, an evangelical pastor, while a graduate student at Andrews University. "We are living in an 'instant' society, when, in a matter of seconds, we have access to data sources on the opposite side of the globe. Out of necessity, we depend upon modern devices to supplement or even replace the functions that our memories served earlier. Information deemed worthy of preservation is committed to writing instead of to memory."[5]

What's most shocking about this quote is that he wrote this in 1999 – almost [25] years ago! What he considered an "instant" society is now the tortoise and today's society is the hare. We have moved from a predominantly oral culture to a written culture and now to a predominantly digital culture. So there could be an argument for why memorizing the Bible or anything is no longer necessary. There no longer remains a burden to retain in memory as much as people used to. And especially in the USA, we have an embarrassment of riches when it comes to accessing God's Word. The world and the Word are at our fingertips, so there no longer remains any need to memorize anything, much less the Bible, right?

Let me channel my "Paul the apostle" voice when I say, "By no means!"

There are two main issues with this thinking:

1. It's that very accessibility that keeps us from actually accessing and treasuring this very precious resource.

2. The majority of the world does not have access to the Bible that the USA does.

The lack of access to Scripture in much of the world even today is astounding. But before I get into that, I want to go back to the invention and development of the printing press. The printing press was invented in 1436. And the very first Bible printed was the Gutenberg Bible printed in 1455. It wasn't until 1611, however, when people had access to the Bible in the common language of their own time – what we know as the King James Bible, which many people to this day still love to read, study, and memorize.

So from the time of Christ in the first 30 years of the first century and to about 95 A.D. when the last book of the New Testament, Revelation, was written some 1300 to 1500 years passed before there was even the possibility of widespread access to personal copies of the Bible. Even then and to this day, high illiteracy rates limit Bible access. This means that for most of Church history, the dominant way for a believer to learn and meditate on the Word for themselves was to memorize it. It allowed them to truly meditate and learn and act on God's Word.

And as I said above, not only are we prone to let technology do the remembering for us today, but we may not use the technology in regards to the Bible at all. I think of how often the things we do the very least are the things most available, the things right in our backyard.

I grew up in Colorado and lived there for 18 years. Colorado offered a wealth of outdoor activities that I could do – hike, bike, go camp, ski, climb mountains, etc. Yet I found myself letting glorious days pass because I thought: "I can do that anytime; I live here. I'll do it another time."

Now I am living in flat Illinois with not a single mountain to climb or ski and no Colorado forests to explore. Oh, how I wish that I had taken more advantage of those opportunities when I lived there! In regards to access to the Bible and Bible resources, there are similarly so many more opportunities that we are not taking advantage of for our spiritual benefit.

But imagine with me for a minute a different scenario. You live in a country where the Bible is either banned or heavily restricted. If you're caught with a Bible, you may be severely persecuted, imprisoned, or killed. That's the reality today for Christians in over 50 countries (25 percent of countries).[6] Or imagine that there is no translated Bible in your own language. Not only can you not have your own personal Bible to read, there are none for you to read. That is the reality for about 128.8 million people who speak 1,680 different primary languages for which there is not yet a written Bible. Imagine you do have access to parts of the Bible, but not all of it. You have neither the full Old Testament nor the full New Testament. That is the reality for 1.45 billion people using 5,509 languages (20 percent of the world population, 75% percent of all languages).[7]

Although we only have to imagine the latter two, I would say it's not all that shocking to think that the first could become a reality for us (specifically for those who live in countries like the USA.) With the current state of the world, we may be headed toward a future where the Bible is banned. Or perhaps we will be imprisoned and left without a Bible as Joshua Summers experienced.

You may not ever be imprisoned for your faith yourself, but many brothers and sisters around the world have little to no access to the Bible and could be punished for even trying to get access to a Bible. Yet you have the privilege at this time in history to have complete access to God's Word, plus numerous commentaries, study Bibles, Bible dictionaries, and other Bible resources. There are more than 100 complete English translations of the Bible and 450 partial translations!

With all that access to amazing resources, I can think of no better way to honor your brothers and sisters around the world and the Lord than to take it all in, to read it, to meditate on it, and to memorize it. Chuck Swindoll says, "I know of no other single practice in Christian life more rewarding, practically speaking, than memorizing Scripture... No other single exercise pays greater spiritual dividends! Your prayer life will be strengthened. Your witnessing will be sharper and much more effective. Your attitudes and outlook will begin to change. Your mind will become alert and observant. Your confidence and assurance will be enhanced. Your faith will be solidified."[8]

To know God through His Word is a powerful experience with benefits that will transform your life and faith, whether you are starting as a new member of God's family or someone long in your faith. In the next chapter, I'll introduce you to the experiences that have made Scripture memory so important to me.

Recall

What do you know by memory? Is it a song? A poem? Your childhood street address? The way you grill a steak or make a pie? When did you learn it?

Reflect

What makes it possible for you to remember the things that you learned? What helped you to memorize them? Are there things you still commit to memory, or do you prefer to look things up quickly online? If you still memorize some things, why?

Go Forward

Make a quick list of all the Bible verses or sections you know by heart. If you'd like to have more of the Word of Truth in hand day by day, pick just one new verse to memorize this week. The list of Scripture Memory Topics at the end of this book might help you choose.

Chapter 2

Why I Began to Memorize Scripture

Scripture has been a significant part of my life for as long as I can remember. From the time I was three — when my family moved to Colorado so my dad could take a lead pastor position at a church in Colorado Springs — I was surrounded by Bible stories. Being the pastor's kid, I grew up in an environment where discussion of the Old and New Testament dominated life at church and home. I knew the answers to all of the Sunday School questions, and thought I knew plenty about God and the Word He gave us.

I also knew that for the entirety of their almost 28-year marriage, my parents had daily devotions together. They would read the Bible and pray together every day. I was only familiar with the term *devotions* and what it meant, but I did not grasp their spiritual purpose and impact. I did not understand why regularly reading and meditating on

God's Word was essential in the life of a believer. That all changed on one particular mission trip.

I was twelve when my church went on a week-long mission to Costa Rica. We were helping a local church repair portions of their building, as well as build a handicap-accessible bathroom. If these repairs were not completed, the government was going to shut down the church.

I was not old enough to help with construction, but what I could do was retrieve a nail or tool or paintbrush for one of the other volunteers. I became the "gofer" kid. During the course of that week, I met one of the primary repairmen, a man named Jonathan, who also served as a translator.

Jonathan was a relatively new member of our church, so I didn't know him very well beforehand. Despite that, Jonathan showed genuine interest in me, and asked many questions about my faith and walk with the Lord. At one point, he asked me if I knew what daily devotions were and if I did them. I told him that I knew what they were because my parents had a devotion time together each day, but I did not do them myself. He then began to tell me about the significant benefits of spending daily time with God and vividly explained how this was key to a thriving "relationship" with the Lord. I do not recall a specific thing he said, but I remember being immensely captivated by the idea that being a Christian meant having a relationship with the God of the universe!

Then Jonathan invited me to join him outdoors for his morning devotions. After spending two hours with him, reading the Word, taking in God's amazing creation, and praying, I was hooked. I knew I wanted to start doing this myself. But like any person wishing to start reading the Bible regularly for the first time, I asked, "Where should I start? How can I do this for myself?" He encouraged me to start by reading two psalms a day, one proverb, and a chapter from one of the gospels. He told me to pray over my time reading the Bible and ask for the Spirit's guidance to understand the passages I was reading. It was during that week that I truly gave my life to Christ, and my love for Scripture was ignited.

I began to eat up the Word every day, taking in everything I was reading. I wanted to grasp more and more about the Bible that I thought I knew so well. Through this time spent with God, the Holy Spirit began to change me within. My bursts of anger became more infrequent, I felt a peace I had never felt before, and I had this desire to love those around me. Other students at school began to notice, but I didn't. They would point out my calm demeanor, the fact that I wouldn't get so upset about things, and that I would show them genuine kindness. It was not until the next year that I understood that it was the Spirit of God changing me from the inside out. By simply spending daily time in the Word, I was growing and being transformed into a more loving and compassionate person by the power of the Spirit.

While I began to thrive spiritually, life turned more challenging mentally and emotionally. My family learned that the breast cancer my mom had endured for seven years moved into her lungs. When the doctors first diagnosed her, they said there was an 85 percent chance she would not live longer than a year due to the aggressive nature of the cancer, but God was incredibly merciful. This time her diagnosis was even more severe, and the doctors said she only had a few months left to live. As she moved into hospice that year, my dad told me that when people go to hospice, it usually means that they are getting ready to pass away. That was hard to bear as a thirteen-year-old kid. And in August of 2010, my mom quietly passed away.

Although I knew she went into heaven that day, my faith was truly tested for the first time in my walk with Christ. It was easy to read the Bible and praise God when things were going well, but suddenly it seemed like my whole world came crashing down. My best friend and my biggest supporter

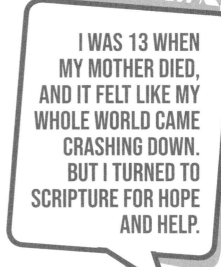

I WAS 13 WHEN MY MOTHER DIED, AND IT FELT LIKE MY WHOLE WORLD CAME CRASHING DOWN. BUT I TURNED TO SCRIPTURE FOR HOPE AND HELP.

was gone. The first major trial of my life had come. By God's grace, I didn't know what to do *other than* to turn to God. I had experienced the richness and goodness of God so thoroughly, and I knew that my mom's greatest desire for me was that I would continue walking with the Lord and trusting Him. As a result, I turned to Scripture for hope and help.

When I did so, James 1:2-4 was the passage I found to be the greatest comfort. It is written, *"Count it all joy, my brothers, when you meet trials of various kinds, for you know that the testing of your faith produces steadfastness. And let steadfastness have its full effect, that you may be perfect and complete, lacking in nothing."* I don't know when or how I discovered this passage, but these are the words that penetrated my heart profoundly during my time of grieving and seeking the Lord. I memorized this verse out of a desire to know these words and have them with me at all times to remind myself of their truth.

It was the first verse I learned and memorized for myself, rather than being taught by Awana or Sunday school. I realized that it was such a comfort to have that verse in my heart, and when I started to struggle with other issues like anger, lust, and other sins, I began to look up specific verses that I could memorize to help me overcome those temptations as well. One of the first verses I memorized after James 1:2-4 was Psalm 119:11; *"I have stored up your word in my heart, that I might not sin against you."* It was then that I realized that memorizing Scripture is truly a great tool that all believers should have as they navigate through life. We can have God's very Word in our minds and immediately on our tongues to help us in all of life's experiences.

After a few years of memorizing individual verses, my hunger for the Word increased. After those early verses in James, I then read the whole chapter. I thought to myself, "This entire chapter is an incredibly powerful passage. I would love to store this up in my heart as well." So, I memorized the whole first chapter of James, all 27 verses. Again, a few years later, I had the desire to challenge myself, so I memorized the entire book of James.

This insatiable longing to really know God's Word is all thanks to the Holy Spirit living inside. Psalm 37:4 says, *"Delight yourself in the Lord, and he will give you the desires of your heart."* As I have taken delight in the Lord, He has given me a desire for His Word, and I know much of it in my heart. Here I am a few years later, writing this book. I truly believe that the passion that God grew in me is not for me alone, but for every Christ-follower.

When I talk to other believers about memorizing Scripture, many of them say that they know it is a great spiritual discipline and they want to do it, but then say something like, "I don't have a good memory," or "I don't have time." This amazing tool and powerful spiritual weapon is usually recognized for its value to us, but many would say they don't take advantage of it enough.

I write this book because I know many of you,

fellow brothers and sisters in Christ, want to memorize Scripture for yourself, but you feel stuck and don't think you can actually accomplish it for one reason or another. Everyone has a reason why they don't memorize Scripture. But I hope and pray that this book serves as a guide and an encouragement to you, demonstrating that you can memorize Scripture, and grow in wisdom, faith and love for the Lord.

After all, the Bible is the only supernatural book in the world. According to Hebrews 4:12, the Word is living and active, discerning our thoughts and intentions. It contains the very words of God given to us that we might be trained in righteousness and equipped for every good work, as it is written in 2 Timothy 3:16-17. Scripture itself tells us *why* it is useful and why we should know it and be able to repeat it to ourselves and others.

Therefore, in this book, I explore some reasons to memorize Scripture. I follow this by addressing common *obstacles* that keep us from memorizing the Word, and how to overcome them. I conclude with the POWER System that anyone can use to effectively memorize Scripture. This system will not just help you memorize Scripture, but as a result of your dedication and commitment to storing up God's Word, it will also help you experience God's power in your life to be a more effective and fruitful follower of Christ, to overcome spiritual battles, and to draw you into a deeper journey with God - one fueled by His Word.

Recall

Has there ever been a time when Scripture really came alive to you? When?

When has your faith been tested by difficult circumstances or personal disappointment?

Reflect

Thank God for having blessed you with His presence through the Word.

Consider how God's Word has supported or comforted you in any of the challenging times you've experienced.

Go Forward

Knowing that life always includes challenges, begin considering how you'll prepare yourself to meet these with God's living presence through the Word of Truth. Think about one of the challenges you're likely to face soon – a difficult coworker, a day so full you don't know how you'll survive, physical pain from a chronic illness, children who are making bad choices. Look for Scripture that will support you. The Scripture Memory Topics and Verses section near the end of this book is one resource; another good one is OpenBible.info.

Chapter 3

Discover Your Why
Making the Case to Memorize Scripture

From the time we are children, we discover that the promise of reward is sometimes all that we need to do something new or challenging.

It's the same with Scripture memorization. While we may generally understand that it's a "good" thing to do, what moves us from thinking about it to actually doing it? I believe the following eight biblical reasons will be enough to convince you that the rewards *far* outweigh the "risk" of spending our time this way.

1. It is God's will for you

God creates each of us out of His infinite love and for His pleasure (Rev. 4:11). He also creates us for His purpose. When we, by faith, put our trust in Christ, and understand what we have been saved from and saved for, our hearts are filled with a desire to fulfill that purpose - loving and pleasing God in return. J.I. Packer once noted, "In Christian living, duty and delight go together…To give oneself to hallowing God's name as one's life-task means that living, though never a joy ride, will become increasingly a joy road."[9] The whole point of the Christian life is to do God's will.

To please God is to do His will, and to do His will is to obey Him. Jesus Himself says, "For whoever does the will of God, he is my brother and sister and mother" (Mark 3:35). There are a few verses in the Bible that explicitly speak of God's will for our lives (1 Thess. 4:3, 5:16-18, 1 Pet. 2:15). It is generally understood that doing the will of God includes reading His Word, praying, being a part of a body of believers to grow in Christian character, and sharing our faith, as well as doing the other works God has set before us.

The reason that we should include memorizing Scripture in our daily lives is that it is also God's will. Psalm 40:8 says, "I delight to do Your will, O my God; Your law is *within* my heart." How could the Psalmist have the law within his heart if he did not have it memorized? When we have the law stored up in our heart and mind, we understand better how to do God's will. Psalm 37:30-31 says, "The mouth of the righteous utters wisdom, and his tongue speaks justice. The law of his God *is in his heart;* his steps do not slip." We can walk on

God's path securely when we are rooted firmly in His Word.

If you are ignorant of God's Word, you will always be ignorant of God's will."

~ **Billy Graham**[10]

2. It brings you healing and comfort

Life is messy. There are incredible joys in life, including the great satisfaction in following after God, but there are also unbelievable heartaches and trials. As I shared in the previous chapter, I dealt with and continue to deal with the loss of my mother. Though she passed away 12 years ago, I still continue to grieve her loss. Yet even in the midst of such trials, we can experience spiritual joy because God is the "Father of mercies and God of all comfort, who comforts us in all our affliction, so that we may be able to comfort those who are in any affliction, with the comfort with which we ourselves are comforted by God. For as we share abundantly in Christ's sufferings, so through Christ, we share abundantly in comfort too" (2 Cor. 1:3-5).

At many painful points in my life, I have found that through my time reading the Word, the Holy Spirit will illuminate a verse or verses that speak to my specific circumstances. When my mom passed away, it was James 1:2-4. When I was struggling with the temptation of sexual sin, it was 1 Corinthians 10:13, and when it was the struggle of feeling unworthy to receive God's grace freely, it was Hebrews 4:15-16. In those moments, I have been comforted not only by the verse, but also by the presence of the Lord as confirmation to me that God sees me in my distress and speaks to me. I respond in praise and thanksgiving, and then commit to storing up that verse in my heart for future moments when I am struggling in a similar situation, so I can recall those verses to bring healing and comfort.

Perhaps you have not experienced that yourself. The Holy Spirit may not always bring to light a specific verse or passage when you are going through a difficult time. In that case, I encourage you to search through the Scriptures to find verses that speak to your circumstances. You know yourself better than anyone else. You know what you struggle with most, whether it is a specific temptation, a particular trial, or other "thorns in the flesh." Scripture is a treasure trove of verses for everyday life. When you are reading, and find a powerful verse that you want to memorize, underline it, and write it down somewhere so you will commit to learning it. If you find it too difficult or time-consuming to search for passages in your Bible, you can check the "Scripture Memory Topics and Verses" section at the back of the book which includes a few of the many resources that can help you. Regardless of how you find them, know that the Word is available to you to bring healing, comfort and encouragement that you might have hope (Rom. 15:4).

Delighting in God's Word leads to delight in God, and delight in God drives away fear."

~ **Dr. David Jeremiah**[11]

3. It brings godly success to your life

Wanting to be successful in life is not a bad thing, as long as it doesn't become an idol – something we value more than we value God Himself. That's the danger of the so-called "prosperity gospel": the idea that it is God's will for Christians to experience financial wealth and physical health. I am not advocating for that. For one thing, it is not biblical, because those who want to live for God are guaranteed troubles (2 Tim. 3:12).

However, experiencing godly success is a different matter. To experience godly success means to know God more intimately. As we draw near to Him, He promises to draw near to us (James 4:8), so that we might experience more of His presence. The more we get to know God, the more fulfilled and joyful we become as we draw close to the Creator of the Universe. In Joshua 1:8, it is written, "This Book of the Law shall not depart from your mouth but you shall meditate on it day and night, so that you may be careful to do according to all that is written in it. For then you will make your way prosperous, and then you will have *good success*."

The idea is not so much being successful in whatever we want to do, but by seeking God and what He wants for us, we will be successful in the life God has uniquely designed for us. All of the principles for success can be found in the pages of the Bible, and by following them daily, we can have true riches that the world can only dream of. I love the way Pastor Craig Groeschel puts it in part two of his "Habits" sermon series:

"The only end goal that ever seems to matter is if I become more like Christ...and if that becomes the driving force of your life, then success is not somewhere out there, but you can be successful when you're obedient to him today...I am obedient because I honored God *today*."[12]

When we meditate on God's Word daily, commit it to memory, and make an effort to do what is written, we will prosper. Christ came to give us life and life in abundance (John 10:10), and this life comes from seeking after God. We have the daily satisfaction of having a relationship with Jesus, and this fuels our success.

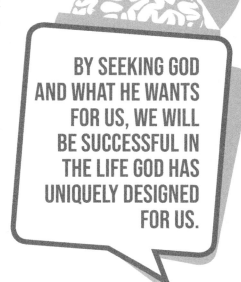

BY SEEKING GOD AND WHAT HE WANTS FOR US, WE WILL BE SUCCESSFUL IN THE LIFE GOD HAS UNIQUELY DESIGNED FOR US.

If our identity is in our work, rather than Christ, success will go to our heads, and failure will go to our hearts."

~ Tim Keller[13]

4. It helps you to overcome sin and temptation

There is nothing more destructive in our life than sin. Sin enslaves the world and keeps us from walking in the Spirit. Sin is the antithesis of a godly life because it is the opposite of righteousness. We are grieved when we sin because we know we have disobeyed God, thanks to the conviction of the Holy Spirit. The desires of the flesh and of the Spirit are opposed to each other (Gal. 5:17), so there is an ongoing battle between our flesh and the Spirit.

But the good news is that we are no longer slaves of sin for "we know that our old self was crucified with him in order that the *body of sin* might be brought to *nothing* so that we would no longer *be enslaved to sin*. For one who has died has been set free from sin. Now if we have died with Christ, we believe that we will also live with him... So you also must consider yourselves dead to sin and alive to God in Christ Jesus" (Rom. 6:6-8,11). Paul continues on in the chapter to say that we are not only no longer slaves of sin, but in fact, on the contrary, slaves to righteousness.

However, this great truth does not mean that we do not stop sinning. We know that sin will always be a struggle as long as we are on this side of heaven. We might sin deliberately, we might sin even when we have good intentions, and we might also sin unintentionally. It's much easier to sin when we forget what God's Word says to us. We may forget what's displeasing to God, and we sin without realizing it. We forget what's pleasing to God, and we sin because of our lack of obedience and action.

In the longest Psalm in the Bible, the psalmist gives a solution to overcoming this struggle with sin when he writes, "I have stored up your word *in my heart, that I might not sin against you*" (Ps. 119:11). Although sin will never completely go away, and we will never remember everything at all times, the more and more Scripture we memorize, the more we will keep away from doing the things that displease God, and do more of the things that please God. Just as with a close friendship or intimate relationship, the more

THE MORE SCRIPTURE WE MEMORIZE, THE MORE WE WILL AVOID DOING THINGS THAT DISPLEASE GOD, AND DO THINGS THAT PLEASE GOD.

we get to know a person, the more we understand that person, what they are passionate about, what pleases them and what displeases them. Our relationship with Christ is founded upon the words that He spoke, for just as He says, "If you abide in me, and *my words* abide *in you,* ask whatever you wish, and it will be done for you" (John 15:7). As with Psalm 40:8, His words cannot abide in us if they are not memorized. And when they are, we will bear much fruit in obedience to God.

 As sin lures the body into sinful action, we call to mind a Christ-revealing word of Scripture and slay the temptation with the superior worth and beauty of Christ over what sin offers."

~ **John Piper**[14]

5. It equips you to refute the enemy's lies and affirm truth

The greatest difficulty of living a godly life is not physical limitations or other people, not even ourselves, but rather the battle "against the rulers, against the authorities, against the cosmic powers over this present darkness, against the spiritual forces of evil in the heavenly places" (Eph. 6:12). Our real test of faith comes from our adversary, Satan. Scripture says that Satan has been "sinning from the beginning" (1 John 3:8) and that he "does not stand in the truth because there is no truth in him. When he lies, he speaks out of his own character, for he is a liar and the father of lies" (John 8:44). He is the exact opposite of truth.

Satan uses our emotions and our feelings often to sway us to believe his lies. When we feel guilty about something we did wrong against God or someone else, and we tell ourselves we are not good enough, it is Satan who is condemning by saying, "That's right. You're not good enough. You can never live up to God's standards, so why bother?" Other times he employs the complete opposite tactic, for example, when we justify something that is wrong and Satan sides with us saying, "It is good to do what you are doing. It's natural to feel what you are feeling. Keep doing it." Regardless of the way he attempts to destroy us, we must contrast his lies with the Truth. The Truth is found in Jesus because He is the Truth.

Jesus set the perfect human example for how we can refute the enemy's lies and affirm Truth when He was tempted by the devil in the wilderness. Each time Satan tries to lure Jesus to sin, Christ uses Scripture. He did not have a physical copy of the law with Him, but He didn't need it because the Truth was in His heart. And because He knew the Truth, He could powerfully refute Satan's lies. Jesus would not allow His physical state or desires to get in the way of holding fast to the Word of God. And neither did He use divine power to rebuke Satan, but He instead chose to identify with us and show us how we can resist the enemy while living with our human limitations. Paul tells us in Ephesians 6:16, "In *all* circumstances take up the shield of faith, with which you can extinguish all the flaming darts of the evil one."

It is undoubtedly harder to accept Truth than to give in to the lies because of our emotions and feelings. We ask ourselves, or moreover, Satan tempts us into asking ourselves, "Does God really love me that much? Is God really with me wherever I go? Does God really have a good plan for me?" However, the compelling aspect of Truth is its immutability. It does not matter what our circumstances are or how we feel; the Truth remains the same. In the same way Jesus did, we must saturate our hearts with Truth so that we can use it to refute the enemy's lies and affirm it in our lives. This matter is so critical that I devoted the entire next section to understanding the lies we believe and obstacles we need to overcome in regards to Scripture memorization.

 I'm not afraid of the devil. The devil can handle me... But he can't handle the One to whom I'm joined."

~ **A.W. Tozer**[15]

6. It equips you to teach and encourage other Christians

The Scriptures we have memorized are a treasure that we don't keep to ourselves. It certainly provides aid when it comes to overcoming one's own struggles as we preach Truth to ourselves. But when we have His Word in our hearts, we are called to use that to minister to other Christians as well. As mentioned in the section on healing and comfort, we know ourselves better than anyone else and what Scriptures we ought to memorize. In this way, just as everyone has their own experiences and gifts within the body, each has different verses and passages that are significant to them. Sometimes, the very verse we have memorized is precisely the verse that another Christian needs to hear in their situation. This is one of the most amazing ways that the Holy Spirit makes His presence known to us: when He brings to mind Scriptures at opportune times. The Scriptures are written for our "instruction, that through endurance and through the *encouragement* of the Scriptures we might have *hope* (Rom. 15:4).

The Word speaks even more explicitly to the value of memorizing Scripture and teaching and encouraging other Christians in Colossians 3:16, when Paul writes, "Let the word of Christ *dwell in you* richly, *teaching and admonishing* one another in all wisdom, singing psalms and hymns and spiritual songs, with thankfulness in your hearts to God." There can be great rejoicing and building up of one another through memorized verses. Thus, the Scriptures are not just meant to be memorized privately and personally, but also spoken out publicly to others. This is not only limited to certain parts of Scripture because "*all* Scripture is breathed out by God and *profitable* for teaching, for reproof, for correction, and for training in righteousness that the man of God may be complete, equipped for every good work" (2 Tim. 3:16-17).

Scripture has value that should not be disregarded, and we must take into consideration the time in which this was written. When Paul wrote these verses, Christians did not have a personal Bible they could read for themselves. The printing press was not invented until the 1440s, so the rare chance that Christians got to read the Bible would not be taken lightly. For Christians to teach and encourage other Christians with Scripture then, they had to have memorized the Word. The Bible is timeless and speaks into our context even now, and that is why it is so powerful. Although we can simply look in our Bible or find a passage using the internet, we should not neglect the discipline that Christians of the past practiced when they wanted to share Scripture with other Christians, and that was to memorize it.

Every day, we have the opportunity to share the Word of God with others. At work, at school, in a restaurant, at the doctor's office — there are lost people wherever we go. If we have stored Scripture we can immediately share the Truth with others, demonstrating the difference that carrying the Bible in our minds can make.

Christians are like the several flowers in a garden, that have upon each of them the dew of heaven, which being shaken with the wind, they let fall their dew at each other's roots, whereby they are jointly nourished, and become nourishers of one another."

~ John Bunyan[16]

7. It renews your mind (and strengthens your brain)

Does anyone else struggle with negative self-talk? The old adage that we are our own worst critics constantly rears its ugly head in my daily life. And the biggest issue with that is that no one spends more time with us than ourselves. Having patterns of negative self-talk and beating ourselves up over what we do can be so destructive to our mental and physical health. No wonder then that Jesus never desired for us to live such a life filled with the torments of the devil and our self-critic without some way to combat it.

The first step is to come to Jesus, who alone can give us rest for our souls (Matt. 11:28-30), and bring every thought captive to the obedience of Him (2 Cor. 10:5). We must learn from Him and take up the whole armor of God to withstand all the evil and extinguish the fiery darts of the enemy (Eph. 6:13, 16). And what we learn from Him is to not be conformed to this world but to be transformed by the renewal of our minds that we may discern by testing what is His will (Rom. 12:2). If we take in His Word, having it actively in our hearts and minds, we will be able, as Charles Stanley says, to "[take] off the old and [replace] it with the new. The old is the lies you have learned to tell or were taught by those around you; it is the attitudes and ideas that have become a part of your thinking but do not reflect reality. The new is the truth. To renew your mind is to involve yourself in the process of allowing God to bring to the surface the lies you have mistakenly accepted and replace them with Truth. To the degree that you do this, your behavior will be transformed."

Another reason to memorize Scripture is the benefit it has on our brains; it actually strengthens them. Psychology professor Victor Garlock states simply that "memorization improves overall memory itself. Memorization increases the size and improves the function of memory-related brain structures. Memorization enhances the neurological flexibility of the brain referred to as neural plasticity."[17] I have found in my own life as I memorize more and more Scripture that I am able to remember other things with greater ability. One example is my ability to remember names. I used to be terrible at remembering names, but I've noticed more recently that I can bring to mind names of people I just met. I think a big reason is because I have learned so many different names throughout the Bible and with all the weird and interesting-sounding names, whether of people or places, I make sure to pronounce them correctly and it sticks more easily. That is just a small example, but I truly believe the more time you spend memorizing Scripture, the more your brain and memory will be strengthened and the more your life will also continually be transformed in amazing ways.

As you pray for the Holy Spirit to make you aware of thoughts that come into your mind that don't line up with God's Word, you'll begin to realize when those thoughts come and you can renew your mind with the Word."

~ **Joyce Meyer**[18]
Treasure the Word

8. It helps you know what you believe.

There is no such thing as blind faith when it comes to believing in Jesus. Though we never get the full picture, and some things appear unclear for us because we are not omniscient, faith in Jesus is based on historical events: the life, death, and resurrection of Jesus Christ from the dead. Paul candidly observes in 1 Corinthians 15:17-19, "And if Christ has not been raised, your *faith is futile* and you are still in your sins...If in Christ we have hope in this life only, we are of all people *most* to be pitied." If Christ was not raised from the dead, we have the most pointless faith. Paul continues, though, declaring, "But in fact, Christ has been raised from the dead, the firstfruits of those who have fallen asleep" (1 Cor. 15:20).

Despite these facts, many of us have a casual understanding of our faith. We believe in Jesus and what He did, but we don't allow ourselves to fully know the weight of what that means and why we believe it. We don't necessarily understand how He is the fulfillment of all of the promises that God made in the Old Testament. We say to ourselves,

"I know the gospel. But I don't need to share it because my pastors do so well at it, and I am not really one for evangelizing." But do we really *know* the gospel? Are our hearts so steeped in the gospel that it oozes out of us, and we can confidently and boldly proclaim what we have allowed to saturate our minds?

God had it in mind since the beginning of humanity that we genuinely know His Word and that we would share it. In Deuteronomy 30:14, it is written, "But the word is very near you. It is in your mouth *and* in your heart *so that* you can do it." When we know the Word, we can do the Word, and we can do the Word because we know the Word. That is why James urges us to "be *doers* of the word and not hearers only, deceiving yourselves. For if anyone is a hearer of the word and not a doer, he is like a man who looks intently at his natural face in a mirror. For he looks at himself and goes away and at once forgets what he was like. But the one who looks into the perfect law, the law of liberty, and perseveres, being no hearer who forgets but a doer who acts, he will be blessed in his doing" (James 1:22-25).

Then, when we truly know it — conceive and adequately assign the right value to it — sharing the Word becomes a natural outflow of this knowledge. Again in Deuteronomy, the Lord instructs His people, "And these words that I command you today shall be on your heart. You shall teach them diligently to your children, and shall *talk of them when* you sit in your house, and when you walk by the way, and when you lie down, and when you rise. You shall bind them as a sign on your hand, and they shall be as frontlets between your eyes. You shall write them on the doorposts of your house and on your gates" (Deut. 6:6-9). This refers to family, but we are also called to always be prepared to share our faith with other believing friends and non-Christians as well (1 Peter 3:15). This is the call of the follower of Christ, so let us obey it with diligence.

 Incline your ear, and hear the words of the wise, and apply your heart to my knowledge, for it will be pleasant if you keep them within you, if all of them are ready on your lips."

~ Proverbs 22:17-18

FIVE

Recall

This chapter offers 8 reasons to memorize Scripture. Take a moment to recall them:

1. It is G____ W___ for Y___.

2. It brings you H___ and C____.

3. It brings G____ S____ to your L____.

4. It helps you to O_____ S__ and T_____.

5. It equips you to R____ L___ and A____ T____.

6. It equips you to T___ and E____ others.

7. It R___ Y__ Mind.

8. It helps you to K___ W___ Y__ believe.

Reflect

Do you think Scripture memory might be valuable for you? Consider the 8 reasons in this chapter – does any one (or more) resonate with you? Are there other reasons that come to your mind? Ask God to help you recognize the reasons He is giving you and to help you ignore the reasons that others might impose on you.

Go Forward

Consider, over the next several days, some Scripture verses that encourage us to memorize the Word. Do any of these speak to your heart and needs?

To find hope: "For whatever was written in former days was written for our instruction, that through endurance and through the encouragement of the Scriptures we might have hope." (Rom. 15:4)

To know how God says to live: "I have stored up your word in my heart, that I might not sin against you." (Ps. 119:11)

To find godly success in life: "This Book of the Law shall not depart from your mouth, but you shall meditate on it day and night, so that you may be careful to do according to all that is written in it. For then you will make your way prosperous, and then you will have good success." (Josh. 1:8)

To experience joy and goodness:

"Whoever gives thought to the word will discover good and blessed is he who trusts in the Lord." (Prov. 16:20)

To live rooted and thriving:
"Blessed is the man
    who walks not in the counsel of the wicked,
nor stands in the way of sinners,
    nor sits in the seat of scoffers;
but his delight is in the law of the Lord,
    and on his law he meditates day and night.
He is like a tree
    planted by streams of water
that yields its fruit in its season,
    and its leaf does not wither.
In all that he does, he prospers." (Ps. 1:1-3)

Chapter 4

Don't Let the Enemy Fool You
You Can Memorize Scripture

Why do some people memorize verse after verse of Scripture when so many don't memorize any at all? Often it happens because people stumble against one of the eight obstacles I'm going to describe that get in the way of Scripture memory.

Some of these obstacles are feelings we have about ourselves. Some are ideas we've learned about what's most important in life. Some are simply lacking specific know-how that would help us memorize Scripture – or anything, for that matter. At the same time, all of these obstacles can be fueled by the one who will do anything to keep you from accessing, reading and memorizing God's Word. He's the one whose entire mission is to keep you as far as possible from truth. No wonder, since he himself is the "father of lies."

If Satan can unconsciously convince you that committing Bible verses to memory is too hard, too time-consuming, or too irrelevant to your daily life, his lies have won. And if the distractions of "the world" and "the flesh" keep you from the treasure that is yours as a child of God, he wins again. Let's shine a light on these obstacles one by one, because they can keep you from all that God intends for you.

OBSTACLE ONE: I DON'T HAVE A GOOD MEMORY.

Unless it's song lyrics or jokes, we don't tend to memorize much these days. Perhaps because the average human attention span is less than ten seconds in this day and age. We are being reprogrammed to handle only short snippets of information at a time, as we scroll through social media posts, videos and other Internet content. How much of that do we actually remember?

As I discussed in the beginning of the book, for thousands of years, we as humans have relied primarily on oral tradition for the information we need. Stories, traditions and other information were passed orally from one generation to another. For example, modern scholars agree and the Bible would show that the Gospels were told long before they were written (Matthew's was the first Gospel written, and it was completed in 43 A.D.). The disciples were sent out to "make disciples of all nations" at least a decade before the life and message of Jesus was available in writing, and that written form would have been just a few handwritten copies, each bearing just sections of God's Word. The oral tradition now, though, is a foreign concept in first-world countries as the primary means of communicating, and as a result so too is memorization for the purpose of sharing knowledge. Now that many of us have access to a hard copy or online version of the Bible, are we more likely to think that a Bible is near and we don't need to memorize it? Could that be why we say we don't have a good memory? Subconsciously we don't think we need to use it? Or we've gotten entirely out of the habit of using it?

If so, perhaps the real reason we believe we don't have a good memory is that we aren't using it enough. After all, we do manage to memorize song lyrics and jokes! Our brains' capacity for memory can grow with practice, much like a muscle can increase in strength with exercise. If I were to ask you to do fifty push ups

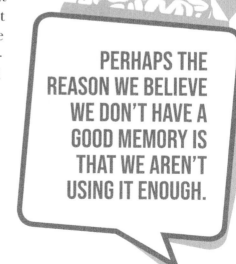

PERHAPS THE REASON WE BELIEVE WE DON'T HAVE A GOOD MEMORY IS THAT WE AREN'T USING IT ENOUGH.

and you hadn't worked out in six months, do you think you would be able to do that many? On the flip side, if you did push ups every day for thirty days straight, do you think you would improve at push ups?

It is the same with memorizing Scripture. If you practiced memorizing Scripture every day, do you think you would improve in your ability to do so? Of course you would! In fact, a study reported in Nature Neuroscience suggests that continued training of a skill beyond learning (called "over-learning") changes our neurochemistry and locks in what we've learned.[19] The more you practice, the more information is moved from short-term to long-term memory.

Practicing Scripture memorization regularly can also improve your general ability to memorize anything, which can have incredibly positive effects on your brain health. Memorizing is an effective way to engage the brain, and that challenge can help stave off cognitive decline. But what about those who are older? Perhaps you are sixty, seventy, or eighty years old and you have never memorized Scripture before and you're wondering, "Is it too late to start?"

During the first few months kick-starting Scripture Alive, my Bible memory and performance ministry, I searched the Internet to find others who also perform Scripture. My goal was to glean from their experience and ask what has and hasn't worked for them. At that time, a California-based pastor reached out to me to say a friend of his gave him my name and website address. He sent me a link to his website and told me that he does Scripture performances as well and would love to connect.

We scheduled a video call shortly afterwards. As we chatted about Scripture performance and what the process was like memorizing Scripture, he mentioned that he was seventy. I asked, "How long have you been doing this? When did you start memorizing Scripture and performing it?" He told me that nine years before, he saw someone perform an entire piece of literature from Homer, which gave him the idea of someday memorizing Revelation and performing it. But he said it was not until seven years later that he started memorizing entire books of the Bible. I was amazed by that.

This pastor was sixty-eight when he started to memorize Scripture. It goes to show that with desire, practice, and consistency, you can develop a good memory and become adept at Scripture memorization, regardless of age.

OBSTACLE TWO:
I DON'T HAVE TIME.

Time is a funny thing. Sometimes we feel that we have too much time or too little time but almost no one ever feels like they have just enough time.

Time is something that continues to move, regardless of our circumstances or how we feel. There is no way to stop time because we have no control over it. One thing we can control is how we *use* our time. I am not saying that we never have obligations or circumstances which keep us from using the time how we prefer. However, the reality is that we find time for the things that are most important to us. Whether it is our job, our family, a sport, a hobby, or traveling, if something is important to us, we will find time for it. Of course this requires sacrifice and effort, since it means we have to cut out or limit something else.

I do also know the reality of different life stages for people where time demands make it difficult to incorporate habits like Scripture memorization into their life. Whether it be a mom of young children or someone caring for their aging parents, it may seem impossible to add anything to your plate. That's why I love what Janet Pope, author of *His Word in My Heart,* says: "I like to tell busy women: 'Okay, you're not going to be able to add Scripture memory to your day. It's already full, so put Scripture memory with things you're already doing.'"[20] She was addressing busy women in this instance, but I believe it applies to busy men as well.

And Katherine Pittman, an author and busy mom, encourages young moms to "use the first free five minutes that you have. It might be that you won't get that until the baby goes down for a quiet time, but at some point you will have five minutes.

And if you give the Lord the first moment...like if you don't give the Lord the first moment, you might not get another moment. I discovered that. I used to think I needed 30 minutes, but when I became a mom, I realized that the Lord knows if I genuinely only have five minutes and...if I genuinely only have five minutes and I come and give the Lord the first five minutes I have...Wow! The Lord meets you and brings some word to life because you're honoring him with your time and he knows that and He blesses that."[21]

We all have time, even if it's just *five minutes* in a day, and the things that mean the most to us will take priority over everything else. This happens on a conscious and subconscious level. If you don't know what takes priority in your own life, examine the things that take up the most of your time, and you will recognize what things matter most to you. You may be surprised by how little or how much time you spend on something or with someone that you believe is important to you.

We may say we don't have time, but the greater issue is often poor time management. We aren't born with natural skills in this area; therefore it's easy to get overwhelmed when we are overbooked. Exhaustion and stress then add to the problem, making it even harder to manage our time.

Here are a few tips for managing time more effectively:

1. Stop and figure out what the root of the

problem is. Do you leave everything to the last minute? Do you put things where they don't belong so it's hard to find them, causing you to waste time? Do you promise too much to too many people? Do you get caught up in a million little things throughout the day? Many times we don't know how to fix the problem because we haven't identified it.

2. Get rid of clutter throughout your house. It makes it much harder to concentrate, causing you to spend precious time getting on track.

3. Identify the "extras" that eat away at your time. You may only spend 20 minutes on social media a day, but that's precious time when you look at how much it costs you in the long run.

4. Do your best to stay focused on the task at hand. It's often hard to get back on track when we stop to answer a text or call that doesn't need our immediate attention.

Often, we do not realize we have more time available than we thought. Therefore, we either have time, and don't want to use it for Scripture memorization, or we have time, but need to replace or limit something else to participate in this spiritual discipline.

You may be surprised to hear that Scripture memorization does not require a lot of time. What if it only took five to ten minutes a day?

We may be in a busy season of our lives when we don't have an hour to spare, but almost everyone has five to ten minutes. Finding that time could mean going to bed five to ten minutes later or getting up five to ten minutes earlier. It might mean reducing time on social media or using the commercial breaks in favorite shows for memorization. There is a way to set aside time for memorizing Scripture. Almost everyone has some amount of discretionary time over which we have control. So let's take those daily moments and commit to doing something that helps us grow more mature in our faith, and become more like Christ.

SCRIPTURE MEMORIZATION DOES NOT REQUIRE A LOT OF TIME— ONLY FIVE TO TEN MINUTES A DAY.

OBSTACLE THREE:
I TRIED BEFORE, BUT IT DIDN'T WORK.

Oh how the world, the flesh and the devil conspire to make us believe this one. We may have attempted to memorize Scripture in some capacity, but found that it was too difficult. Perhaps a pastor or teacher assigned it as part of a sermon series or Bible study, and we found that we couldn't stick with it. Maybe after attempting it once or twice and failing, we came to the conclusion that we are incapable of memorizing Scripture. Let me ask a cliché question; how many times did Thomas Edison try unsuccessfully to create a lightbulb? Did he stop trying after he failed more than 1,000 times?

My dad likes the acronym FAIL ("First Attempt In Learning)" to describe the almost inevitable lack of success when a person begins to learn anything new.

There is a lot to be said about failure, in fact it's a hot topic for motivational speakers. This one from Denis Waitley is particularly accurate: "Failure should be our teacher, not our undertaker. Failure is delay, not defeat. It is a temporary detour, not a dead end. Failure is something we can avoid only by saying nothing, doing nothing, and being nothing."[22]

While I likely don't agree with everything this man taught, this comment is powerful. We fail when we do nothing. Attempt is never a failure! Scripture memorization takes effort and consistency, just like any other activity that we want to undertake. Perhaps memorizing does not come naturally to you, but that does not mean you cannot get better at it over time.

Another reason I believe you may not have been able to succeed in memorizing is you tried to do it with your weakest learning style. I will cover the VARK model of learning styles in the next section, but it is vital to know what your best learning style is. Perhaps someone showed you the way that they memorize Scripture, which was to hear it audibly on their phone and to repeat it back. Then they repeated that process ten times for each verse. So you went home and tried that and were frustrated by the fact that you couldn't recall the verse the next day. The difficulty may not be due to your lack of ability to memorize, but that you are more of a visual learner who needs to see what you're memorizing or maybe you do better with movement and learn through doing. Switching to a learning style that is more effective for you is likely to go a long way in helping you to succeed in memorizing.

It could also be that it takes you longer to memorize Scripture and you might need to take a slower, more comprehensive approach. The pastor in California I connected with says he has a seven-month memorization process, but he does not begin to memorize until the third month. He spends the first two months just reading the passage every day. Then by the time he starts to memorize, he is so used to the passage that he can infer what comes next. This makes the memorization process much easier for him, and by the time seven months is over, the text is deeply embedded in his heart.

OBSTACLE FOUR:
I DON'T KNOW HOW TO DO IT.

The real issue at hand here is how to memorize anything at all. Although it is entirely possible to commit a significant portion of Scripture to memory, the question becomes, "How do I start? What do I do?" Again, while you may have memorized a verse or two as part of a weekly Bible study, making a habit of Scripture memorization may sound more challenging. You may search for quick tips and tactics, but it's helpful to know that memorizing will be different for everyone. We have different learning styles that affect how we respond to different types of teaching and methods of learning.

According to the VARK model of learning styles, people may be Visual, Aural, Read/Write, or Kinesthetic learners.[23] The first step in developing a plan to memorize the Word is to know which one you are and to put that type of learning to the test. Personally, I am a read/write and aural learner. I respond well to hearing myself repeat the words as I look at the passage. Reading and re-reading as I practice portions works for me. You may be an aural learner and respond well to listening to the passage over and over. Use that to your advantage. Record yourself or have it ready to go on the Bible app and listen to it while you're driving, doing dishes, or working out.

The read/write learner does better if they read the Scripture and write it on note cards or paper. The act of writing it down helps you remember, then you can review what you've written for re-inforcement. The kinesthetic learner can process information and remember better if he or she is engaged in a physical activity at the same time. These are the "hands-on" people who learn best by doing. I know a little girl who absorbs her kindergarten studies better if she is manipulating an object in her hand—like a stress ball.[24]

Think about what has always worked best for you — in school, at work and elsewhere. You can capitalize on your learning style to develop an amazingly fruitful Scripture memorization practice. Do not be afraid to experiment. Whether you are a visual, kinesthetic, auditory, or some other type of learner, it is possible to memorize Scripture, but it is crucial to figure out the method that works for you and stick with it.

The hardest part of Scripture memory for most people is remembering the chapter and verse references. Here's a tip that often helps: Whenever you recite a verse or passage, always start with the verse reference, then the verse itself, and then the reference again. That will really help it "stick".

OBSTACLE FIVE: I DON'T KNOW WHICH SCRIPTURES TO MEMORIZE.

It can seem very daunting to look through the Bible and try to decide where to start. Fortunately, it really does not have to be that complicated. Whether you have been a Christian for one year or forty years, I am sure that there have been specific verses that friends, family, pastors, or other Christians have said, or that you have read, which really spoke to you. You listened to or read a verse and thought to yourself, "Wow, I really needed that," or "That is powerful and encouraging." Or perhaps you have a specific struggle or struggles in your life, whether it's a sin or a troublesome circumstance, that you want to address with the Truth.

That is an excellent place to start. Ponder the verses that mean something to you in your spiritual walk. If you haven't already stored them up in your heart, commit to memorizing those verses.

If you cannot think of a verse, why not use a search engine to help you choose? You can search, "What does the Bible say about" and type in what you want to find. Often, OpenBible.info will be the first option that shows up.

OpenBible.info is a tremendous resource that gives you verses that speak to the topic you're searching for. But as mentioned previously, make sure to check out the "Scripture Memory Topics and Verses" section at the back of the book with verses to pick from. For instance, if you struggle with forgiving others, I recommend a number of verses, including Matthew 6:14-15: "For if you forgive others their trespasses, your heavenly Father will also forgive you, but if you do not forgive others their trespasses, neither will your Father forgive your trespasses."

Other favorite resources include the *Treasury of Scripture Knowledge* by R.A. Torrey, and the app "Bible Notes," which is the mobile version of the book. This book contains the most exhaustive listing of biblical cross references available anywhere – over 500,000 – and parallel passages. It is a great Bible study tool in and of itself, and I highly recommend it. With tools like these and taking time to think of those verses that are meaningful to you, you will be on your way to choosing the Scriptures you want to start to memorize.

OBSTACLE SIX:
I DON'T FEEL LIKE IT.

This could be interchanged with the phrases "I don't want to" or "I have no interest in it." Not many of us would be quick to admit these out loud, because as believers we are called to treasure God's Word and carry it with us. You may love Bible study, but dislike trying to memorize portions. There are many things in life that we don't feel like doing or don't want to do. Many of us don't like going to work, but we do it anyway because we need to be able to provide for ourselves and/or our families with the money we receive.

I exercise multiple times a week, but there are many times when I don't feel like going to the gym because I'd rather sleep more, or I am a little sore, or (insert other excuse here). However, I know that it is good for me, and it keeps me healthy and strong. Even though I don't always want to do it, I know it will be better for me in the long run.

As we covered in the last chapter, there are many reasons why to memorize Scriptures, and we need to take these into consideration in regards to this obstacle. There are more benefits to memorizing Scripture than not to, and sometimes it takes that pushing through of our emotions and feelings of disinterest to press on to continue with it. Once we begin to see progress and change, we will be more likely to continue. Early success fuels future success in the same way that people are more likely to stick

MEMORIZING SCRIPTURE IS NOT JUST A CHORE OR EXERCISE BUT VALUABLE TIME SPENT WITH GOD.

with a diet plan if they see pounds coming off in the first week.

My sincere hope is that you quickly come to experience memorizing Scripture as a vital spiritual activity that is not just a chore or exercise but valuable time spent with God. This time will help you grow in your faith, your understanding of God, and your ability to love Him and others.

Paul writes in 1 Timothy 4:8, "While bodily training is of *some* value, godliness is of value in *every* way, as it holds promise for the present life and also for the life to come." And when we delight ourselves in the Lord, He will give us the desires of our heart (Ps. 37:4). What that verse means is that our desires become aligned to His will and what He wants for us, and yet it is still something we want. As we grow closer to God, our awareness of what He has given to us grows so we may better glorify Him and make Him known.

As for those who say they have no interest, also consider the verse above. If you are a believer in Jesus, the God of the universe, then His words should be of great interest to you. What the Scriptures tell us about Him and what He did is incredibly significant for our lives. He was the only perfect human being, and every word of His proves true. They are not the empty words of a family member or a friend who promises you things time and time again and never comes through. These are the words of a faithful Father whose words will not return to Him empty but will accomplish what He purposes and succeed in the thing in which He sent them (Isa. 55:11), and "every word of God proves *true*" (Prov. 30:5). It's a joy and privilege to know them and treasure them in our hearts.

OBSTACLE SEVEN:
I DON'T THINK IT MATTERS.

If we have access to a physical or online Bible, why would we think we need to memorize Scripture? If it's literally at our fingertips, why would we ever concern ourselves with committing it to memory? If it's just an "add-on," it probably doesn't matter, right?

Here again I think the enemy of our souls would love us to think this way, especially in light of how little access much of the world has to the Bible. While in America we don't worry about the Bible being banned or illegal, we do need to understand that's the case in other countries. It's in those places that believers routinely memorize large portions of Scripture in order to share it with others who don't have access to a Bible. Should God give you the opportunity to live or travel in those countries, the only portions of the Bible you will carry are the ones you have committed to memory. With "cancel culture" on the rise in western civilization, can we be sure that we will always have God's Word physically or digitally available to us? It may sound alarmist, but it's not beyond the scope of our Enemy and those who follow him to limit or eliminate access to the Bible here as has happened elsewhere. It's easy to see why it's essential for all believers to hide God's Word in their hearts in case we see those days. If censorship like this does not happen in your lifetime, then praise God. If it does, you and the worldwide church can be ready.

OBSTACLE EIGHT:
I THINK IT SOUNDS LEGALISTIC.

Being a Christian is not about doing good works. Our faith is not dependent on what we do but rather what Christ has done. His finished work on the Cross satisfies the penalty all of us deserve for our sinfulness, and we have only to receive the gift of faith that God has given us. With that being said, this great gift should stir in us a desire to grow in our faith and obey God. He calls us to glorify Him and make Him known. He wants to have a personal relationship with us. He wants us to know His story and His promises to us. This calls for faithful conduct and intentional time spent with Him and our fellow brothers and sisters in Christ.

We often associate living a godly life with the reading of the Word, prayer, sharing our faith, and being a part of a local body of believers, and for good reason.

If you are already spending time reading the Word, talking to God in prayer, wanting to listen to Him and hear the Word in church, perhaps you're thinking, "Why should I also memorize it?" In addition to all of the other reasons I gave in the previous chapter, I would add that we should have a passion for memorizing God's Word because Jesus did. His life on earth offered the greatest example of drawing nearer to God through the memorized Word of God. While Jesus believed that the Pharisees were legalistic in how they memorized, lived and promoted the law, His knowledge of His Father's Word was far deeper and purposeful. He used the Word to counter the arguments of the Enemy (Matt. 4:4-11). He quoted the Word when He taught what God expects of God's people (for example, Matt. 5:21-42, Matt. 19:16-20). He quoted the Word when He explained how He knew that the dead will rise to a new life (Matt. 22:31-32, Mark 12:26-27, Luke 20:37-38). And He often quoted the Word when helping people sort through their confusion about making good choices (Matt. 12:7, Matt. 15:1-6,

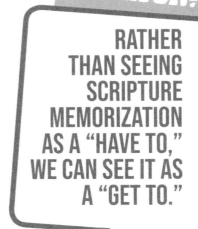

RATHER THAN SEEING SCRIPTURE MEMORIZATION AS A "HAVE TO," WE CAN SEE IT AS A "GET TO."

Matt. 22:37-40) and their uncertainty about who He was (Luke 4:17-19, 21; Luke 22:37).

Rather than seeing Scripture memorization as a "have to," we can see it as a "get to." Especially if we grasp that soaking up the Bible and referring to it in our minds throughout the day can transform our lives. We are privileged to have the opportunity to literally carry the life-giving, life-changing and powerful Word of God with us wherever we go. I for one am thrilled to do so. It fuels me and motivates me to fulfill God's call on my life. Why not join me?

FIVE

Recall

Have you ever tried intentionally to memorize anything? Perhaps the multiplication tables or vocabulary in a foreign language? Were you successful? How much do you still remember? Why do you think the parts you remember have stuck in your mind?

Have you ever tried to memorize Scripture? Was it similar to or different from other experiences of memorizing things? How? What was easier and harder? Do you still remember any verses?

Reflect

What are some ways you want to change your life? Do you believe God wants to be part of making those changes?

Go Forward

Look for Scripture verses that describe how God wants for you some of the changes you want for yourself. You'll find some ideas in the section of Scripture Memory Topics near the end of the book. Choose just one verse to commit to memory this week. Use the POWER system (next chapter) or other memory techniques that have worked for you.

Chapter 5

How to Memorize Scripture
The POWER System

I want to finish off by sharing a simple but effective system that can be used for fruitfully storing up God's Word. The key to all of this is the value you place on filling your heart with the Truth and the effort that you are willing to invest to make this part of your life. As with any skill or activity, Scripture memorization takes practice and effort to improve. See these as a formula of five steps that you can use over and over as you memorize more and more verses, passages, and books of the Bible.

P – Pick, Plan, and Pray

Pick Your Passage

While it may sound obvious, choosing the passage you are going to memorize is the first step to any Scripture memorization. You have to consciously decide what you are going to spend time learning. Unless you are in Awana, a fellowship like Navigators, or are assigned memory verses for a class, the verses you memorize will be ones that *you want* to memorize. You can expand your choice from a verse or two to an entire chapter, story or book. Maybe you want to learn large portions of the Bible or to hide Bible stories in your heart so you can perform them for groups. Or maybe you will concentrate on memorizing verses related to a topic that's important to you. That works as well.

This is a simple tip, but nonetheless necessary. Whether you want to look up verses about wisdom, love, overcoming anxiety, or God's promises, Scripture contains a wealth of verses, passages, and stories that speak about these topics. If you aren't quite sure where to start, check out the Scripture Memory Topics and Verses section in the Resources section at the back of the book. There are more than 30 topics with over 200 verses to get you started. Hopefully you will see that this is not just about memorizing so you can memorize, but about internalizing verses that can help you grow in your Christian life and become a more effective and fruitful follower of Christ. This is by no means an exhaustive list, but this list should give you a sufficient number of ideas for you to be able to pick from, which will allow you to move forward to the planning step.

Plan It Out

After you have chosen the passage, it is now time to plan it out. The old adage is used often for a reason: if you fail to plan, you plan to fail. This is where the discipline piece of "spiritual discipline" comes into play. But you will thank yourself for creating a tangible plan that you can put into action.

The pick section determines **WHAT** you are memorizing; the plan section determines the **HOW, WHERE, WHEN**, and **WHO**.

HOW

I would encourage you first to write the verse(s)/passage down. Put it in your journal or create a Word document so you have something down on paper or print to refer to. Then make sure to note how many verses you will be memorizing. You may already know this especially if you picked a single verse or a three-verse section, but if you decide on a chapter, make sure you know how many verses are in the chapter.

Once you know the number of verses, decide on how many verses per day/week/month you want to memorize. It doesn't matter whether you're a veteran memorizer and can do five verses a day or you're a beginner and can do one verse a month, choose a pace that is comfortable for *you*.

Once that's finished, you will then be able to determine how long it will take. Just take the number of total verses you're memorizing and divide it by the number of verses per day/week/month. For example, if you picked out Psalm 23, which has six verses, and decided on doing one verse a month, six divided by one is six months. It will take six months to learn Psalm 23. Write/type that down where you put the passage and now you have a plan for how you're going to memorize your passage.

WHERE

Okay, you've been motivated or the Lord has stirred up your desire to memorize Scripture. You've taken the first steps by picking the passage you want to memorize, you know how many verses you are doing, and how long it's going to take you. Great! *Where* are you going to memorize? While you're in the middle of getting your kids ready for school, right? Or while you're in the midst of a big project at work? While you're watching TV?

While I am being facetious about the first two, the third one may seem like a good idea, but I would advise against it, at least for when you're *first* memorizing a passage, because the best place to memorize is in a place where you are alone and have limited distractions.

There is a time when you can do memorization anywhere but that's best left for the review section when you are working on retaining it. But for this part, you want to find a spot in your house or room where you can devote 100 percent of your attention and focus to memorizing. If it is a spot that usually has things that can easily distract you (like a device or in a place that gets a lot of people traffic), either move the distracting things out of the specified area or find a spot that doesn't have those distractions.

WHEN

Just as important as it is to find a place where you can be focused and devote your attention to memorizing is doing it at the time when you're most alert. It's as simple as determining what the best time of day is for you – when you are energized and have a good recall.

For many people, it may be in the mid-morning right after that first cup of coffee. Perhaps it's during the afternoon when you get a second wind. If you're like me, perhaps you are an early bird and can do it right when you get up. It's crucial to find a time that works best *for you*.

I love to do it in the morning because that's both where I can be alone with limited distractions (no one is up and I have the quietness of the morning) and I have the most energy because I was just able to sleep for seven or eight hours beforehand. I also love having my quiet time with the Lord first thing in the morning, which comes from my desire to "seek *first* the kingdom of God and his righteousness" (Matt. 6:33). And the beautiful thing about storing up God's Word in your heart is that you are spending time with Jesus. So, I get to double up my quiet time (i.e. devotions) with my time of memorizing Scripture.

WHO

You've determined the where and the when, so now it's about determining who will be your accountability partner. This is pivotal. You may have all the desire in the world and have even picked a passage and set out a place and time to memorize, but without someone joining you in the activity or at least checking on your progress, you can easily get discouraged and quit after a week or a month.

I imagine that one of the major reasons why someone who tried to memorize Scripture before but thought they couldn't do it was because they went into it without a partner. You need someone else to join in the fray with you, so you can mutually challenge and encourage one another as you grow in your knowledge of the love of God and His Word.

Ideally, you and your partner will be memorizing the same or similar material (like verses on the same topic, two short psalms or chapters from an epistle) and can meet together weekly or bi-weekly to recite the passages you're memorizing and share what God has been teaching you. It can be your spouse, a close friend, or perhaps someone that you don't know as well at church that you invite to join you in memorizing a psalm or a short chapter. Regardless of who it is, make sure you have someone helping you and encouraging you in your journey.

One of the most tangible ways you can keep that accountability is schedule a meetup with your partner to recite your passage after the deadline. So, let's say you memorize a three-verse passage. You've determined to memorize one verse a week, so you will memorize it in three weeks. Since you meet once a week or once every other week, that following week, the fourth week, you can recite your passage during your normal meetup time. Again, ideally your partner will be memorizing the same passage or something very similar, so you can both have the same scheduled meetup to share your passages and encourage one another through the blessing of sharing the Word of God with one another.

Pray For Empowerment and Understanding

The last part of this step is to consciously make God part of your team. Pray about the commitment you're making. You are not just learning random words by heart, you are learning God's Word, which is eternal and powerful – it changes and transforms us. You get to invite the Holy Spirit to be a part of the process – ask Him for His help to enable you to store up His Word in your heart. Jesus says in John 14:26 that the Helper, the Holy Spirit, "will teach you all things and bring to your remembrance all that I have said to you."

This is amazing! If you are desiring to store up God's Word in your heart, the Holy Spirit is ready and willing to help you in that endeavor. The Holy Spirit is on our side and He will bring into remembrance what we have been taught. This is why I say memorizing Scripture is never a waste of time. Even if you've memorized just a collection of verses, a small passage, or a small chapter in the past and you've forgotten it from a technical standpoint, i.e. you couldn't recite it word for word at this moment, the Holy Spirit can and will still use in the future what you've memorized in the past. Don't underestimate the Spirit's ability to bring into mind a Scripture you've stored up at an opportune time to minister to you, to someone else, or to a group. Be expectant that every word of Scripture you memorize in your lifetime will bear fruit. How can I say that so confidently? Because I know that God's Word will never comes back void. It will accomplish what God purposes for it (Isa. 55:11).

But you don't want to ask for the Holy Spirit's help to enable you just to memorize but also to *understand* what you're memorizing. I love how

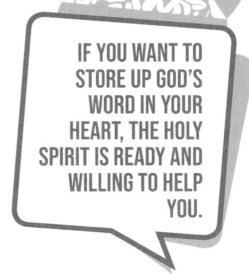

IF YOU WANT TO STORE UP GOD'S WORD IN YOUR HEART, THE HOLY SPIRIT IS READY AND WILLING TO HELP YOU.

Aaron House, founder of Piercing Word, emphasizes not just memorizing the words, but memorizing the *thoughts* of the words. You truly can't memorize what you can't understand. But that's what's beautiful about verses like John 14:26, which reveals that the Holy Spirit is our Teacher. He is the one who will give us proper insight into the passage we are memorizing.

O – Overcome Excuses

Just because we are aware of the excuses we use, or we know why we should or should not do something, does not mean we always follow through. If you are human, then you likely struggle with this too at times. There is a reason that Scripture memorization is considered one of the spiritual disciplines; it takes discipline and it nurtures our spiritual growth.[25]

We must be dedicated to it and choose to overcome excuses. There will be many times we don't feel like doing it, but that does not mean we should stop doing it. Just as with going to the gym, eating healthy, or writing a book, it is easy to tell yourself that you can do it later, or think of reasons to do the opposite. Take this tip as a challenge to review the preceding chapters on *why* to memorize Scripture and the *obstacles* we face in it to help you to overpower any excuses. And make sure to stick with your plan that you made in the Pick, Plan, and Pray step.

For me, as a Scripture performer, my plan for memorizing a passage is based on the date of my performance. If I book a performance eight weeks in advance and I have 50 verses to memorize, I give myself six weeks to memorize the passage so that I have two weeks of space before the performance. This gives me time to review and solidify the passage so that I am in command of it when I perform. So, 50 verses in six weeks is about 8 verses a week, a little over one verse a day. So, I go through the Pick, Plan, and Pray step and write down each verse that I will memorize each day and I commit to working on it every day. It is easier to keep at your Scripture memory plan when you set a goal and break it into smaller, achievable tasks so you can enjoy success as you work toward your bigger goal.

As I discussed the importance of accountability with a partner, another way to keep accountability and overcome excuses is to memorize as a group. Whether you ask your church small group about memorizing something together or you join a small group that already has a Bible memory initiative, this can be a helpful and motivating way to get over the hump when it comes to putting Scripture memory into action.

The double portion is that you can study the passage/book together and memorize the passage/book together. Then you can set up a system where either one person recites a verse/verses for a string of weeks or you all recite it together at the end of a certain time. This is a tangible way of encouraging one another daily and building one another up (Heb. 3:13, 1 Thess. 4:18, 1 Thess. 5:11). Just as God created us to live and serve communally, there can be a great richness and blessing of memorizing His Word communally as well.

W – Work On It Daily

As has been said before, consistency is key. It is easy to think that you don't have a good memory, and you don't have time to memorize Scripture, when you are not working on it regularly. Not actively engaging your brain in memorizing something will undoubtedly diminish your ability to remember it, and if you are not making time to memorize Scripture, you will fill up the time that you would be memorizing with something else. Again, what's most important to you will be shown in what you spend your time doing, so you will make time for what is important to you.

When we decide to prioritize Scripture memorization in our lives, we have the time to work on it. Daily practice is most effective for long-term recall, in the same way that regular study of school work beats cramming for exams if you'll need the content over the long term. Daily practice may seem daunting at first, but it doesn't require long blocks of time. In fact, when it comes to memorizing anything, it is most effective in short bursts of concentration. That's because our brains can only handle so much at once. Eight-time World Memory Champion Dominic O'Brien relies on short bursts of concentrated effort to achieve his remarkable memory feats.[26]

I would suggest to you that five minutes a day is all you need to practice and continue memorizing Scripture. If you want to do more than that, I encourage you to practice the fifteen minute principle. If you want to memorize for an hour, memorize for fifteen to twenty minutes and take a break. Do something else and then come back to it for the same amount of time and repeat that once or twice more depending on how long you plan to do it. It does not matter the length, as long as you work on it daily.

Digital marketer Joshua Summers has a great video on YouTube called "7 Bible Memory Mistakes I've Made (& how you can avoid them)" and one of those mistakes is not making it a daily habit. He says, "I've found that if I don't make it a daily habit, then one day of not memorizing turns into two, turns into three, and all the sudden, I just kind of forget about it for a

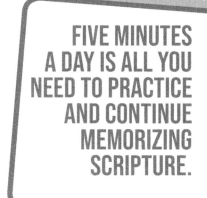

FIVE MINUTES A DAY IS ALL YOU NEED TO PRACTICE AND CONTINUE MEMORIZING SCRIPTURE.

week or two. If it's not a daily habit – and it doesn't have to be long. I'm not even saying 10, 20, or 30 minutes. Even just five minutes sitting down and memorizing new Scripture, so not just reviewing, but memorizing new Scripture, that has been key to me. And that is a mistake I've made in the past, not doing that."[27]

We similarly view the five minutes as key to making it a daily habit. Don't put pressure on yourself to make it this big thing. And even if it doesn't seem fruitful and you think that you did bad, that's okay. Joshua interviewed Pastor Scott Stonehouse discussing how to build Scripture memory habits and I love how succinctly he puts it: "A bad day reading the Bible is better than no day. A bad day working on Scripture Memory is better than no day."[28]

What a principle for spiritual life! Whether it's five minutes or fifty minutes or 500 minutes, when you are making an effort to honor God with your time and grow closer to him each day, He will honor you and will use that to bear fruit in your life. Don't neglect creating that daily habit of working on Scripture memory because it will also help you press on and not get away from the practice of it. If you make it as easy as possible to implement into your daily routine, you will be more likely to practice it.

E – Express It

The beautiful thing about Scripture is that it is all true. The stories are real stories with real people who had real emotions. They would have emphasized certain things at different times, and the inflection in their voices would have conveyed different tones. The writers of non-narrative books, like the books of wisdom and the epistles, wrote in ways to highlight different elements of their subject matter. Although we cannot fully know how people in the Bible said what they said or fully understand how the writers felt about their content, through careful studying of the text and through the leading of the Spirit, we can interpret and understand the meaning and intent of a passage.

What kind of emotions is the writer or character conveying in the verses you are memorizing? Express it! Express your enthusiasm and energy for the subject material. All of this will enhance your brain's ability to remember the passage word for word. This is when we can put the VARK model into action. Over these next pages, I am going to give you some practical and engaging techniques to creatively memorize Scripture, which will in turn allow you to express it in a fun and memorable way. You will see that I simplify this creative process into a memorable phrase.

When I first learned the medium of oral interpretation (i.e. performing memorized Scripture word for word from the Bible) for a Communications Elective at Moody Bible Institute, I was in a class, aptly named "Oral Interpretation." In that class, we learned the different techniques for how to engage with a phrase or a verse. The professor said we can either *see it, say it*, or *be it*. To make an easier connection with the VARK model of learning styles, the last one will change from be it to *do it*.

Visual/Read & Write

Write it

This is a simple, but effective way to engage visually with whichever Scripture you are memorizing. By writing it out, you are connecting your brain with your hand. This creates new pathways in the brain which helps you to deeply embed the verse in your heart and mind. It's no wonder then that God affirms this practice:

"And these words that I command you today shall be on your heart. You shall teach them diligently to your children...You shall bind them as a sign on your hand, and they shall be as frontlets between your eyes. You shall *write* them on the doorposts of your house and on your gates" (Deut. 6:6-9).

For those familiar with The Navigators, their Topical Memory System standardized the model of carrying pocket-sized notecards in a notecard holder. Writing your memory verses down on notecards with the verse reference on one side and the verse on the other side is classic, but you can also write them in a notebook, on sticky notes, a whiteboard, or whatever you have accessible to you.

Type it

Similarly to writing, this is a great way to connect your eyes, your hands, and your mind. Some people prefer writing on their laptop or tablet as opposed to writing it by hand, so this is a great technique for these people.

I use this technique in a slightly different way. As someone who memorizes whole stories and books of the Bible, you can imagine it would be quite time-consuming to type (or write) out every word. So, instead, I will copy and paste the passage and print it out. Then I will fold it up small enough for it to fit in my back pocket. This way, I am still utilizing the visual style of learning as I look at the passage

and memorize it. Then, by always having it in my pocket, whenever I am out and about and I am trying to recite the passage but am struggling with a word or phrase, I have immediate and easy access to it.

Draw it

You don't have to necessarily be artistic to be able to draw the Scriptures. It can be as easy as writing a verse with different colors, shapes, and simple images associated with the words. For example, with Proverbs 3:5-6, the first phrase is to trust in the Lord "with all your heart." A simple association is to draw a couple of hearts around the word "heart" or put the word inside a bigger heart. This easily connects the word with the thought/ meaning of heart which in turn makes it more memorable. Although it can take some time and effort with different colors and shapes, you can also make it more basic and take a less is more approach. But the reality is almost anyone can draw the Scriptures no matter how simple.

On the other hand, you can be quite artistic and creative with detailed drawings of ideas or

images to really connect the words of a verse and the meaning of it. One of my favorite examples I've ever seen was a word picture of 1 Corinthians 10:31, which says "So whether you eat or drink, or whatever you do, do all to the glory of God." The artist drew a set of realistic hands palm-up. In the left hand are three almonds representing the word "eat" and in the right hand is a small amount of water representing the word "drink." It's a visually striking image that helps you picture the meaning of the verse. But both simple renderings of word pictures and detailed ones are strong examples of word pictures that will help Scriptures go from your head to your heart.

Visualization

There are quite a few ways to incorporate visualization into memorizing but I will present to you two. The first is to create visual images in your mind. Associating a verse with unique and interesting visual images that stand out in your mind will make it that much more memorable. Creating something memorable in your mind in connection with a verse will help you to better recall it. For example,

with Psalm 34:8, you could imagine yourself as a chef at a restaurant testing out a new recipe that looks amazing and you take a bite (taste and see that the Lord is good.)

The second way, known as the Memory Palace (or Method of Loci), is similar, but you link the new verses you want to learn to a place you know well in your memory (like your childhood home). This method has been used since before Jesus was born as a way to store up huge chunks of information. Many world memory champions employ this technique, and it is considered one of the most effective ways to memorize Scripture. You can use it whether you're a pre-teen or senior. In brief, it allows you to connect different parts of the information you want to memorize with specific locations in a familiar place – perhaps the various rooms in your childhood home, or the workout stations at your favorite gym. Josh Summers gives an excellent overview in a video you can review online.[29]

Game it

You may be surprised to hear this, but Scripture memorization can actually be fun! It

is still a spiritual discipline, so it does take effort and planning, but there is much opportunity for fun. This comes in part from the joy of storing up more of God's truth in your heart for yourself and others, but can also come in the form of different games to engage your brain and more effectively memorize verses.

One simple way is to erase words as you go. You start with writing out the whole verse and saying it out loud. Then you erase a few words and try saying it again. Continue until the verse is blank. Another game (which is a whole memory system in itself) is the first letter technique. You write the first letter of each word in a verse which works as a visual aid to help you memorize. You could write it on a note card to take with you on the go or even buy or create your own memory wristbands for verses you want to memorize and meditate on.[30]

Apps

This could be categorized under "Game It," but apps encompass more than just games. They have review tools, databases to store the verses you've memorized, and give different

practical tips. Whether it's Verse Locker or The Bible Memory App or a different app, there are a good number of apps that can help you effectively memorize and review Scripture. Most are free. Some involve a cost but are well worth it. The Bible Memory Goal website has reviewed top memory apps, and I trust their recommendations.[31]

Sing it

Just like the drawing technique, this one does not require you to be a musician or even a great singer. These techniques are meant to be used for your own personal memorization. The key is to pick techniques that you enjoy. So, even if you know you don't sing well, but you enjoy singing, then by all means do it! Whether it's singing a verse to a familiar tune (like "Mary Had A Little Lamb") or your own

tune, you'll find that combining music with Scripture can really help those verses you memorize stick.

If you're a parent with especially young kids, I highly recommend checking out Songs for Saplings. It is a holistic educational tool that teaches Biblical truths (Scripture along with doctrine) to children, currently in three languages with the goal of offering many key languages for children worldwide. The music makes these timeless texts stick longer and go deeper, forming students' hearts and prayers.[32]

Songwrite it

In contrast to singing it, this one does require a certain level of musical skill to add this to your Scripture memory tool belt but not as much as you might think. Abigail Houston, founder of Melodically Memorizing, has a deep love for music and has been singing since she was little. She began to create her own Scripture songs after discovering that her youth pastor's simple, guitar-accompanied melodies made it easier for her to remem-

ber Scripture. What I love about her songs is that she creates them word for word with the Scripture references. So a song of one to two verses might be only 30-60 seconds long; a bigger chunk might run 90-180 seconds. I highly recommend this approach for those who want inspiration to create their own songs or to use songs to learn Scriptures.

Record it

Some definitely do not like the sound of their own voice and can't imagine recording themselves saying a verse. You may be in that boat. And that is perfectly okay. Again, pick tools you enjoy. But you can also still utilize this by having someone else record the verse. Maybe you really like your spouse's voice; ask them to record it for you. Then that way you get to hear their beloved voice while meditating on and memorizing God's Word – a win-win!

This can also be a very effective tool for those who are busy/in busy seasons. One of the lies the enemy tells us is that we are too busy to memorize Scripture and when we don't make Scripture memory a priority, it makes

it that much harder to commit to creating a lifestyle habit out of it. But this is an excellent option to counteract that busyness because you can combine it with other activities you're doing already. So, once you record it, you can listen to it and repeat it during your commute to work, on your lunch break, at the grocery store, making dinner, etc.

Accents or Voices

Now we're getting into my kind of territory. Having a theatrical performance background and doing solo dramatic Scripture presentations, I have just a little experience in needing to create different voices for characters. And I find it just so entertaining playing around with a variety of accents and voices. The thing is that being alone with limited distractions, you can give yourself permission to look and sound silly. No one is watching you or recording you. I would challenge you to step beyond your comfort zone.

Even if you don't go so far as to do a New York accent when reciting John 3:16 or as a game show host reciting 1 Thessalonians 5:16-18, experiment with emphasizing dif-

ferent words and changing the inflection in your voice. By allowing yourself to engage with Scripture in this way, you may find yourself gaining new insight into the meaning of a passage and you will better lock in Scripture by not repeating it with the same cadence and rhythm over and over again.

Act it

Speaking of new insight, acting the Scriptures is an even greater tool to understand and explore a passage. I haven't done a book report in a long time, but whenever I would read a book in school, I always remember discussing the tone of the author. We would discuss what they were feeling and what they were trying to convey. Their tone can change throughout the course of the book, and we had to pay attention to when that happened. And what better way to understand that than to read it out loud?

In regards to Scripture, a good example is the drastic difference in tone between the letters of Galatians and Philippians. Although both letters are written by Paul, are written

around the same time, and are addressing a first century church, their tones are not even remotely the same. But you might miss this if you were to just read these letters silently or read it audibly but in monotone. So do yourself a favor by acting the Scriptures. And a simple way to act it is to try different emotions (happy, sad, afraid, etc.) or intentions (to persuade, to impress, etc.)

Recite it

At the end of the day, you may be someone who does not consider themselves a creative person nor are you inclined to be creative when it comes to auditory learning. If that is you, there is nothing wrong with doing the tried and true method of repeating verses out loud. As an actor, I learned that you have three friends when it comes to learning your lines: 1) Repetition 2) Repetition and 3) Repetition. The more you say the Scripture out loud, the better you will be at repeating it without needing to look at it.

DO IT

KINESTHETIC

Hand motions

Hand motions are similarly effective to the musical ways in learning Scripture because they engage a variety of elements. And just as it's common to have kids learn a song while also doing hand motions, you can easily combine motions with music to cement Scripture in your own mind that much more easily. Creating gestures can really be effective because it involves doing something physical and anyone can create motions that will be memorable for themselves. (This is great to do with your kids!)

It's not rocket science; there is no right or wrong way to do it. To make it really easy, let's look at Ephesians 6, the armor of God passage. There are already memorable visual images included in the passage so the only thing to do is to add actions to those images. Verse 17 says, "and take the helmet of salvation, and the sword of the spirit, which is the word of God." In this instance, I would be as literal as possible. I would bring my hands forward and pretend to take the helmet from a helmet rack and put it on my head. Then I would "grab"

the sword by crossing my right hand over to my left hip and taking it out of the scabbard. Then I would finish with opening up both my hands to represent the Bible. See? Simple, easy, memorable.

Dance it

By nature, this technique is not really an isolated one; it would most likely be a combination of music, hand motions, and physical movements, which is excellent. As mentioned in the beginning, it is optimal to use all three learning styles. And like the music and hand motions, this can be as complex or as simple as you want it to be. If you are a dancer or dance choreographer, I say dance and choreograph your heart out. This could even be a good group activity. There are times where small groups memorize a chapter or book together, so it could be that you have a group of Christian friends who love to dance and you do an entire dance set to a chapter or book of the Bible. Although this may not be for most people, this is certainly a unique way to memorize Scripture.

Act it out

The difference between this and "Act it" is hopefully clear. You are not just verbally emoting, but you are using your body to bring a passage to life. I strongly recommend this for any Bible story you want to memorize; they are the easiest types of passages to use this technique with because of the narrative, the characters, the emotions, etc. Many of the stories give us the exact blocking of a scene as well. For example, Daniel 3:19-21 (in the New International Version) clearly states, "Then King Nebuchadnezzar was furious with Shadrach, Meshach, and Abednego...He ordered the furnace heated seven times hotter than usual and commanded some of the strongest soldiers in his army to tie up Shadrach, Meshach, and Abednego and throw them into the blazing furnace."

I don't have kids, but I can imagine how fun it would be to organize a family "Act it out" of Luke 2 for Christmas, or to act out the David and Goliath story (1 Sam. 17) together. And what's powerful about combining movement with Scripture is that your brain connects the words, the sound of the words, and the move-

ments, allowing you to remember the story more easily. There have been times I present a story where I forget the line but remember the next movement and that triggers in my brain the next verse.

Go for a walk

For me, it's always a plus when I can be active while memorizing Scripture. I tend to do this often when I am memorizing a new passage. There is a beautiful park close to my house with a big pond and several walkways, so in the morning when I am most alert, I'll take a nice 45-minute walk around the park and memorize throughout. If you're an avid treadmill user, the same concept can apply, and if you can really multitask, you could get in a jog or a workout. In this case, it would probably be best to use the "record it" technique where you listen to it and say it out loud.

And there is something to be said for the effect that exercise can have on your memorization. You will enhance your ability to learn something by being active. Personally, I know that it causes me to be more alert and

focused and I can better engage with a passage as opposed to sitting down.

Final Note

We've talked about discovering your best learning style so you can most effectively memorize Scripture. But you should also notice: learning styles crossover. The best teachers use all three learning styles, so you should also seek to incorporate the other two learning styles with the primary one you like to use. This will hopefully not only be a very effective way of storing up God's Word in your heart, but also a very engaging and fun way!

R – Review It

Whether you have a great ambition to memorize many verses, chapters, or books of the Bible, or desire to simply have a few, it can be hard to work on every chosen passage daily. However, you might be thinking, "Why couldn't I? I am not memorizing a lot at once." But consider the context of your life. As Scripture memorization is integrated into your life, the more years go by the more verses you will have memorized. Even if you memorize just one verse a week for every week of the year, that would be fifty-two verses. Now think forward five or ten years. You would have learned more than 500 verses in ten years. If you only memorize one verse a month, but you did that for ten years, you would have 120 verses memorized!

The point is that as you make Scripture memorization a part of your regular life, eventually you will come to a point when you cannot work on every individual verse/chapter/book every day.

You might also be working on an entire book for an extended period of time, so the individual verse and smaller passages will take a back seat to your daily practice. That is why it is crucial to review. Having memorized passages stored somewhere in that online database or physical filing system comes in handy. Apps are perfect for review. They do almost all the work for you in terms of which Scriptures to review and when.

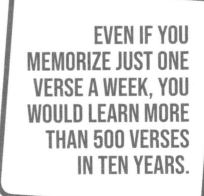

EVEN IF YOU MEMORIZE JUST ONE VERSE A WEEK, YOU WOULD LEARN MORE THAN 500 VERSES IN TEN YEARS.

But I want to make sure to bring up the two vital components of reviewing: they are *Reinforce* and *Retain*.

Reinforce

When you first pick a passage, plan out how many verses to do a week/month, where and when you're going to memorize, who you're going to have as an accountability partner, and you commit to that plan by overcoming excuses, working on it daily, and expressing it, and you come to the point when you have memorized the complete passage, that is a live, one-time process. It's totally new Scripture you have memorized, not one you memorized a month or two years ago.

Once you've memorized something for the first time, that's when you go into the reinforcement stage. As you used 100 percent of your attention and focus for that first part, you want to do the same for this stage. It should come directly after you've memorized. So, if you memorized three verses in three weeks and you finished on a Friday, on Saturday you should start to reinforce. This is a time to recite the passage from beginning to end to ensure you have it down. That's why you need all your attention and focus. You can do it by yourself or you can have your accountability partner with you to check for errors.

Whether you've memorized one verse or a whole chapter, recite it as reinforcement every day for at least a week. Anything above a chapter (or 25 verses), I would recommend a month. This will really help you in the process of moving what you've memorized from your short-term memory to your long-term memory.

Retain

After you have recited your passage for at least a week up to a month, you should have it to a point when you're in command of it. You can say it in front of anyone and could do it even with distractions. You don't need to worry about focusing on it 100 percent because you know it frontwards and backwards. And that is where the blessing and joy of memorizing comes from. Why? Because you will retain these words you memorized and can access them anytime and anywhere! You can do it while multitasking (whether you're taking the dog for a walk, doing dishes, driving in the car, taking a shower, etc.)

These words are now truly yours and you get the rest of your life to rehearse the wonderful truths of these words. Now you get the chance to truly meditate on

> THE BLESSING AND JOY OF MEMORIZING IS THAT THE WONDERFUL TRUTHS OF THESE WORDS ARE TRULY YOURS FOR THE REST OF YOUR LIFE.

and marinate in these Scriptures. How could the psalmist in Psalm 1 meditate on God's law day and night? In an ancient culture where there were no light switches or cell phone flashlights, it is implied that the psalmist had these words in his heart so that he could meditate on them. And what was that like for him? It was a *delight*.

I hope that knowing God's Word in your heart and having it ready on your lips is a delight and joy for you. Whenever I retain a passage, I pray that I would be able to understand the words I recite in a fresh way, and that the Lord would speak to me through them and give me a fresh joy and delight in them. I ask that the truth of the words would penetrate my heart even deeper so that I might be more in awe of God. For I desire to treasure the words of His mouth more than the portion of my food (Job 23:12).

REPEAT THE PROCESS

You've reviewed by reinforcing and retaining, and now I challenge you as a final step to repeat the process. I'm not just talking about repeating the verse/passage you memorized, but once you've gotten to a point of being able to retain a passage, take your next step by choosing a *new* passage and go through the whole process again. Be blessed in picking a new passage, planning it out, praying over it, overcoming excuses in your commitment, working on it daily, expressing it, and reviewing it. And be blessed as you continue to store up God's Word in your heart!

Recall

Take a moment to recall the elements of the POWER system for memorizing Scripture:

P _____

O _____

W _____

E _____

R _____

Reflect

Where do you want your life to demonstrate more of God's power? Is it in steadfastly working toward a godly goal? Graciously responding when irritated or opposed? Encouraging others – even the ones you envy? Ask God to guide you to places in His Word where you could find more of His power. The Scripture Memory Topics section in this book could help. Another resource is OpenBible.info.

Go Forward

Choose just one Scripture to pray over your own life every day this week. Here are a few possibilities::

Psalm 25:4-5

Psalm 101:2-3

1 John 2:6

2 Corinthians 5:17

Next Steps and Final Thoughts
Be Blessed in Your Doing

I've told you that I began memorizing Scripture after my mom had passed away. First I memorized James 1:2-4, and that eventually became my life verse. A few years later, I memorized the entire first chapter of James because it was so powerful. I especially loved James 1:22, which speaks about being "doers of the word and not hearers only." I have always wanted to be someone who didn't just hear God's Word but truly does and applies His Word for life transformation. I didn't want to be like the man in James 1:23-24 who looks at himself in a mirror and then walks away and immediately forgets what he is like.

James 1 continued to shape my life. I first memorized Scripture because of the hope and encouragement I received from James 1:2-4. Then, when I struggled with anger and lust as a young teenager, I knew that these temptations were not of God but from my own desire (James 1:13-15). That drove me to say no to sin and to act on the things I was memorizing (James 1:22). And now, through Scripture Alive, I hope to inspire and equip others to memorize Scripture so that they also may be doers who act on God's Truth (James 1:25).

That's why I have created the POWER System. It's not just so you'll learn skills to memorize Scripture but so you can grow stronger in your relationship with Christ and be able to act on the things that you are memorizing. You will thus fulfill the call of James to be a doer of the Word. As a result, you will be *blessed by God in your doing.* In this way, you can become a POWER-FUL witness of Christ's work, a person who will:

> *Faithfully share it,*
> *Use it in prayer,* and
> *Live it out.*

Faithfully Share It

When we memorize the Word, we need to share it. This implies the significance of continually doing that. We want to be faithful to our God, for we know He is always faithful to us. His words are, in fact, life to us (Prov. 4:22) and a lamp to our feet and a light to our path (Ps. 119:105). In 1 Samuel 12:24, Samuel exhorts the Israelites to "fear the LORD and serve him faithfully with all your heart. For consider what great things he has done for you." We know that we will never be entirely faithful to Him at all times, but we are always striving for faithfulness.

To be faithful to God's Word, we cannot keep it just to ourselves, but are to declare His Word to others because we are called to do it. Before Jesus ascended into heaven, His final commandment was that His disciples "make disciples of all nations, baptizing them in the name of the Father and of the Son and of the Holy Spirit, *teaching them* to observe all that I have *commanded you*. And behold, I am with you always, to the end of the age" (Matt. 28:19-20). Therefore, let us hold fast His words, keep His commandments, and live (Prov. 4:4).

Use It In Prayer

There is also such power in being able to pray Scripture for yourself or for others. To pray God's Word back to Him is something that has shaped my praying life significantly. Whether it's a simple prayer to start the day like "Make me to know *your way*, O Lord; teach me your paths. Lead me in *your truth*, for you are the God of my salvation; for you I wait all the day long" (Ps. 25:4-5) or in times of temptation to say "I will ponder the way that is blameless. Oh when will you come to me? I will walk with *integrity of heart* within my house; I will not set before my eyes anything that is worthless" (Ps. 101:2-3), to have the Word ready on my lips in prayer encourages me so much. It truly allows me to be transformed by the renewal of my mind. I am meditating on His Truth and am reminded of His Truth as I pray it.

I also can't tell you how many times the Lord has used me to pray Scripture over others. As a donor appreciation representative at Moody Bible Institute, I talk with a lot of ministry partners from every demographic you can think of – young adults, retired couples, great grandmothers and grandfathers, Hispanic, Asian, Black, White, single, married with young kids or teenagers, empty nesters, you name it. And every single one of them is going through radically different circumstances, positive and negative.

And when I call them on the phone, I get to hear about their circumstances and I get to pray for them. It is an absolute joy and privilege to pray for them and when I pray for them, the Holy Spirit brings into mind so many Scriptures. Oftentimes, it is the exact Scripture that they need to hear or it's simply encouraging for them to hear the Word of God in prayer. That's the thing about utilizing Scripture in prayer: it's not hard to recognize the Word of God. When someone hears Scripture being prayed, they can sense it even if they don't remotely know where it is in the Bible. The Word has power; it has authority; it sustains one who is weary and blesses those who hear it. Don't neglect the use of Scripture memorization to enrich your prayer. You will be blessed by it and will bless others with it.

Live It Out

The culmination of being a powerful Christian who knows God's Word is living it out. John writes in his letter, "Whoever says he abides in him [God] ought to walk in the same way in which he [Jesus] walked" (1 John 2:6). Jesus walked in obedience to His Father during His time on earth. As these truths carry spiritual weight, they sanctify us. As our outer self is being wasted away, "our inner self is being *renewed* day by day" (2 Cor. 4:16). And "if anyone is in Christ, he is a *new* creation. The old has passed away; behold, the new has come" (2 Cor. 5:17). The Holy Spirit in us gives us new life that we might live for God, for before we were dead in our trespasses, but now we have been made alive in Christ.

As a thanksgiving and praise to God, we live for Him. When we have stored up His Word in our hearts, our goal is to live it out. The two greatest commandments given by God and affirmed by Jesus are to love God with all your heart and with all your soul and with all your mind, and to love your neighbor as yourself. If we keep Christ's commandments, we will abide in His love, just as He kept the Father's commandments and abides

OUR GOAL IN STORING UP HIS WORD IN OUR HEART IS TO LIVE IT OUT.

in the Father's love (John 15:10). John expounds upon this further in his letter when he writes, "whoever *keeps his word*, in him truly the love of God is perfected" (1 John 2:5). To live a godly life means to hold fast to God's words and obey them in love. For if we love God and love others, we fulfill the rest of the commandments (Matt. 22:40).

Final Thoughts

You've now read through some of the most important reasons why every believer should make a habit of memorizing Scripture. I've done my best to help you see the obstacles that Christians face when memorizing. I finished off by sharing the POWER System to give you practical tools for Scripture memory success. There are other reasons for memorizing Scripture, and obstacles that may keep us from it, but the important thing is to recognize that Scripture memorization should be a vital part of our relationship with Christ, just as important as reading and studying the Word, praying to God and for others, sharing our faith with unbelievers, being a part of a church, and living as a faithful disciple in all that we do.

To memorize the Word is simply an enhancement to the reading and studying you are already doing, but it's an enhancement that will be invaluable in your spiritual life. The most painful moments in my life, when I fall short and feel utterly worthless, are also the sweetest, most life-giving moments when the Holy Spirit brings into mind those truths I have stored up in my heart. The truth of God's Word has the power to restore you and set you free. In my time memorizing the truth that God's grace is sufficient for me (2 Cor. 12:9), and that I can find grace anytime I am in need (Heb. 4:16), I've learned to better grasp the depth and love God has for me.

So, I ask you: why not take a little extra time to make sure the words that will challenge, encourage, and teach you are with you always, so that you might be more "transformed by the renewal of your mind, that by testing you may discern what is the will of God, what is good and acceptable and perfect" (Rom. 12:2)? It is easier to please and obey God when we know what He said is good and beneficial and what is bad and sinful. The Word is meant to instruct us, correct us, and train us so that we might be equipped for good works. These good works do not save us, but they do demonstrate the saving faith we have in Jesus Christ.

For "no one has ever seen God; if we love one another, God abides in us and his love is perfected in us" (1 John 4:12). And when we love, "let us not love in word or talk but in deed and in truth" (1 John 3:18). To love in truth is to love by His Word because His Word is Truth (John 17:17). So, let us treasure His words and feed on them, for when we thirst for Him, we can say that "My soul will be satisfied as with fat and rich food, and my mouth will praise you with joyful lips" (Ps. 63:5).

SCRIPTURE MEMORY RESOURCES

As you begin or continue your Scripture memory adventure, you may find some of these resources helpful. They include good starting places for memorization – Bible verses by topic, short Bible stories, plus Bible chapters and even books that you could consider memorizing. I've also listed some of the organizations and books that help with Bible memory skills, plus others who, like me, perform Scripture to help build up the Body. These are the resources you'll find:

- 200 Topical Verses to Memorize

- 40 Great Bible Stories to Memorize

- 30 Great Chapters of Scripture to Memorize

- 10 Short Books of the Bible to Memorize

- Organizations, Performers, and Books

200 TOPICAL VERSES TO MEMORIZE

Roman's Road to Salvation I Rom. 3:23, Rom. 6:23, Rom. 5:8, Rom. 10:9-10, Rom. 8:1

Assurance of Salvation in Christ I John 1:12-13, John 3:16, John 14:6, 1 John 5:11-13

Prophecies of Christ I Gen. 3:15, Ps. 110:1, Is. 7:14, Is. 9:6, Is. 53, Dan. 2:44, Mic. 5:2, Zec. 9:9

Faith/Trust in God I Ps. 23, Ps. 37:5, Ps. 56:3, Prov. 3:5-6, Rom. 10:17, Eph. 2:8-9, Heb. 11:1,6

Heaven I Matt. 6:19-21, John 14:2-3, Phil. 3:20-21, Heb. 11:16, 2 Pet. 3:13, Rev. 21:4, Rev. 22:1-5

God's Word I Deut. 6:6-9, Josh. 1:7-8, Ps. 1:1-3, Ps. 119:11, Rom. 15:4, Col. 3:16, 2 Tim. 3:16, Heb. 4:12

God's Will I Rom. 12:2, Eph. 5:16-17, 1 Thess. 4:3, 1 Thess. 5:16-18, Heb. 10:36, 1 Pet. 2:15, 2 Pet. 3:9

Obeying God I Deut. 28:1, 2 Chr. 7:14, Luke 11:28, Rom. 13:8, Jam. 1:22-27, 1 Pet. 1:14-16

God's Blessings I Num. 6:24-26, Ps. 31:19, Ps. 34:8, Is. 40:31, Eph. 1:3, Phil. 4:19, Jam. 1:17

God's Promises I Josh. 1:7-8, Matt. 6:33, Rom. 8:28, 2 Cor. 1:20, Eph. 2:10, 1 John 1:9

Mercy I Ps. 25:6-7, Lam. 3:22-23, Luke 6:36-37, 1 Tim. 1:13-16, Tit. 3:5, Jam. 2:13, 1 Pet. 1:3

Grace I Rom. 6:14, Rom. 11:6, 1 Cor. 15:10, 2 Cor. 12:9, Eph. 1:7, Eph. 2:8-9, Heb. 4:16

Christ-likeness I John 15:4-5, Rom. 12:9-21, 2 Cor. 4:16-17, Eph. 5:1-2, Phil. 2:3-5, 2 Pet. 3:17-18

Life Verses I Ps. 55:22, Jer. 29:11, 2 Cor. 5:17, Gal. 2:20, Phil. 4:13, Jam. 1:2-4 (My life verse)

Prayer I Matt. 6:6,9-13, John 15:7, Phil. 4:6, 1 Thess. 5:17, 1 Tim. 2:1-4, Jam. 5:16, 1 John 5:14-15

Sharing Your Faith I Matt. 28:18-20, Acts 1:8, Acts 4:12-13, Rom. 1:16, 1 Pet. 3:15-16

Sin | Ps. 119:11, Prov. 28:13, Rom. 6:11-12, 2 Cor. 5:21, Jam. 4:17, 1 Pet. 2:24, 1 John 1:8-10

Temptation | Matt. 26:41, 1 Cor. 10:13, Eph. 6:10-18, Heb. 2:18, Heb. 4:15, Jam. 1:13-15

Sex | Gen. 2:24, Matt. 5:28, Rom. 13:13-14, 1 Cor. 6:18-20, Col. 3:5, 1 Thess. 4:3-5, Heb. 13:4

Anxiety/Worry | Is. 26:3, Is. 40:31, Matt. 6:25-34, John 14:27, Phil. 4:6-7, 1 Pet. 5:6-7

Fear | Deut. 31:6, Josh. 1:9, Ps. 27:1, Ps. 34:4, Ps. 56:3, Prov. 29:25, 2 Tim. 1:7, Heb. 13:6, 1 John 4:18

Trials/Perseverance | John 16:33, 1 Cor. 15:58, 2 Cor. 1:3-4, Jam. 1:2-4, 1 Pet. 1:6-7

Overcoming Depression | Ps. 9:9, Ps. 34:17-18, Ps. 143:7-8, Lam. 3:22-23, 2 Cor. 1:8-9

Overcoming Anger | Ps. 37:8, Prov. 15:1, Prov. 29:11, Eph. 4:26-27, Col. 3:8-10, Jam. 1:19-20

Forgiveness | Ps. 32:1-5, Ps. 103:10-12, Is. 1:18, Matt. 6:14-15, Matt. 18:21-22, Eph. 4:32, 1 John 1:9

Work/School | Prov. 12:24, Eccl. 9:10, 1 Cor. 10:31, 1 Cor. 15:58, 2 Cor. 10:5, Eph. 6:5-8, Col. 3:23

Self-Control | Prov. 25:28, Dan. 1:8, 1 Cor. 9:24-27, Gal. 5:22-23, Tit. 2:11, 2 Pet. 1:5-7

Love | Matt. 22:36-40, John 13:34-35, Rom. 13:8, 1 Cor. 13, 1 Pet. 4:8, 1 John 3:16-18, 1 John 4:8

Serving | Josh. 24:15, 1 Chr. 28:9, Matt. 20:26, Mark 10:45, Rom. 12:11-13, Gal. 5:13, 1 Pet. 4:10-11

Thanksgiving/Worship | Ps. 100:4, John 4:24, Rom. 12:1, Eph. 5:20, 1 Thess. 5:18

Wisdom | Prov. 1:7, Prov. 2:6, Prov. 12:15, Prov. 15:22, Ps. 90:12, Dan. 2:20-23a, Jam. 1:5, Jam. 3:17

Generosity | 1 Chr. 29:9,14,17, Prov. 11:24-25, Luke 6:38, 1 Cor. 16:2, 2 Cor. 9:6-7, 1 Tim. 6:17-19

Money | Deut. 8:17-18, Prov. 13:22, Prov. 22:7, Eccl. 5:10, Matt. 6:24, 1 Tim. 6:10, Heb. 13:5

40 GREAT BIBLE STORIES TO MEMORIZE

Stories are such a wonderful part of the human experience. Stories connect us. Stories teach us. Stories move and inspire us. It's little wonder then that 70 percent of the Bible is narrative. Our Creator created us as relational beings and what better way to relate than the real stories of others? And He Himself is a storytelling God who gave us the greatest story ever written—that He loved the world so much that He gave His only Son to pay the penalty for the sin that separates us from Him so that we might be reconciled to Him.

So consider these stories to memorize. Naturally, this is not a comprehensive list as there are many more stories in the Bible that help build our faith. But these are some of the most popular and famous stories in the Bible. They are ones that could be easily memorized and retold to family and friends, or your small group, or your church. The stories vary in length from nine verses (The Tower of Babel) to fifty-eight verses (David and Goliath). They are listed in order of appearance in the Bible, starting in the book of Genesis and ending in the book of Acts.

Adam & Eve (Genesis 2:15-25, 3:1-24)

Cain & Abel (Genesis 4:1-16)

The Tower of Babel (Genesis 11:1-9)

Abraham Tested To Sacrifice Isaac (Genesis 22:1-19)

Joseph & His Brothers (Genesis 37:1-36)

The Cupbearer & the Baker (Genesis 40:1-23)

Joseph Interprets Pharaoh's Dreams (Genesis 41:1-40)

Moses' Birth (Exodus 1:8-22, 2:1-10)

Moses & the Burning Bush (Exodus 3:1-15)

The Fall of Jericho (Joshua 5:13-15, 6:1-6:27)

The Birth of Samuel (1 Samuel 1:1-28)

The Call of Samuel (1 Samuel 3:1-20)

David & Goliath (1 Samuel 17:1-58)

David & Bathsheba (2 Samuel 11:1-27)

Elijah & the Widow (1 Kings 17:1-24)

Elijah & the Prophets of Baal (1 Kings 18:17-46)

The Lord Appears to Elijah (1 Kings 19:1-21)

Elisha Heals Naaman of Leprosy (2 Kings 5:1-27)

Nebuchadnezzar's Dream (Daniel 2:1-49)

Daniel's Three Friends Tested (Daniel 3:1-30)

Daniel in the Lions' Den (Daniel 6:1-28)

The Baptism & Temptation of Jesus (Matthew 3:13-17, 4:1-4:11)

Jesus Walks on the Water (Matthew 14:22-36)

The Parable of the Sower (Mark 4:1-20)

Jesus Feeds Five Thousand (Mark 6:32-44)

The Birth of Jesus (Luke 2:1-40)

The Good Samaritan (Luke 10:25-37)

Jesus Changes Water Into Wine (John 2:1-10)

Jesus Teaches Nicodemus (John 3:1-21)

Jesus & the Samaritan Woman (John 4:4-42)

Jesus Heals A Man Born Blind (John 9:1-43)

Jesus Raises Lazarus (John 11:1-46)

Jesus Reinstates Peter (John 21:1-25)

Peter Heals a Crippled Beggar (Acts 3:1-20, 4:1-4)

Saul's Conversion (Acts 9:1-19)

Peter's Miraculous Escape From Prison (Acts 12:1-17)

Paul & Silas in Prison (Acts 16:16-40)

Paul Preaches in Athens (Acts 17:16-34)

The Shipwreck (Acts 27:1-44)

Paul in Malta (Acts 28:1-10)

30 GREAT CHAPTERS
OF SCRIPTURE TO MEMORIZE

Although there is a great value in memorizing individual verses, I love to encourage and challenge others to memorize whole passages of Scripture. There is something wonderful about seeing a whole passage in context and being able to take time to meditate on multiple verses that are directly connected. You get the flow of the thought, and it is such a blessing to be able to repeat and rehearse an entire chapter to yourself.

So whether or not you are ready for this now, consider these chapters as potential Scriptures to store up in your heart in the future. Chapters range from Genesis to 1 John and are in order of appearance in the Bible. I've included several psalms because 1) they are short 2) their poetry deeply connects with human emotions and experience 3) you probably already know verses from these well-known chapters, so familiarity will ease the process of memorization. Length ranges from 6 to 51 verses.

Genesis 1 (31 Verses)

Exodus 20 (26 Verses)

Deuteronomy 6 (25 Verses)

Psalm 1 (6 Verses)

Psalm 23 (6 Verses)

Psalm 27 (14 Verses)

Psalm 46 (11 Verses)

Psalm 51 (19 Verses)

Psalm 84 (12 Verses)

Psalm 91 (16 Verses)

Psalm 139 (24 Verses)

Isaiah 53 (12 Verses)

Matthew 5 (48 Verses)

Matthew 6 (34 Verses)

Matthew 7 (29 Verses)

John 1 (51 verses)

John 15 (27 Verses)

Romans 8 (39 Verses)

Romans 12 (21 Verses)

1 Corinthians 12 (31 Verses)

1 Corinthians 13 (13 Verses)

Ephesians 2 (22 Verses)

Ephesians 4 (32 Verses)

Ephesians 6 (24 Verses)

Philippians 3 (21 Verses)

Philippians 4 (23 Verses)

Colossians 3 (25 Verses)

James 1 (27 Verses)

1 Peter 1 (25 Verses)

1 John 1 (10 Verses)

10 SHORT BOOKS
OF THE BIBLE TO MEMORIZE

Many may not be ready to memorize whole books, but if you are already memorizing short chapters (15-25 verses), most of these books are essentially three or four short chapters long. When you break it down like that, it is more doable than you might think.

These books range from 25-155 verses. If you were to memorize just one verse per week, you could learn each of these books in as little as six months (Philemon and Jude are 25 verses each) and at the very maximum three years (Ephesians is the 155 verse book.) But what if you did a book in your small group or in your church? If you divvied it up between friends or several people in a group, you could each memorize a section and complete as a team the whole book. Think of the blessing and enrichment you would experience together as you stored up God's Word communally! Either way, consider these short books as potential Scriptures to hide in your heart. Books are in order of length in verses, with two Old Testament and eight New Testament books.

Philemon (1 Chapter, 25 Verses)

Jude (1 Chapter, 25 Verses)

Titus (3 Chapters, 46 verses)

Jonah (4 Chapters, 48 Verses)

Ruth (4 Chapters, 85 Verses)

Colossians (4 Chapters, 95 Verses)

Philippians (4 Chapters, 104 verses)

1 John (5 Chapters, 105 Verses)

James (5 Chapters, 108 verses)

Ephesians (6 Chapters, 155 verses)

ORGANIZATIONS, PERFORMERS, AND BOOKS

Author Jeremy Kluth's website, videos, and bookings for events, retreats, chapels, and more:

🌐 ScriptureAlive.com

Find Scripture Alive on YouTube - Facebook - Instagram

Organizations, Schools and Training

Awana Bible Clubs for churches, Christian camps and more:

🌐 Awana.org

BibleMemory.com Bible memory app, verses by topic, helpful tips and tools:

🌐 BibleMemory.com

Bible Memory Goal, Website and YouTube Channel to inspire others to start (or restart!) memorizing Scripture:

🌐 BibleMemoryGoal.com

MemVerse.com Online Bible memory verse training program and online community:

🌐 MemVerse.com

National Bible Bee Scripture memory training and competition:

🌐 BibleBee.org

Scripture Memory Fellowship:

🌐 ScriptureMemory.com

Songs for Saplings, Music Resources to help teach kids Scripture through song:

🌐 SongsforSaplings.com

Word by Heart YWAM Kona Training School:

🌐 YWAMKona.org

Scripture Performers, Bible Actors and Groups

Aaron House, Piercing Word,
🌐 PiercingWord.org

Abigail Houston, Melodically Memorizing,
🌐 MelodicallyMemorizing.com

Marquis Laughlin, Acts of the Word Ministries,
🌐 ActsOfTheWord.com

Max McLean, Fellowship for Performing Arts,
🌐 FPATheatre.com

Matthew Moore, Lamp & Light Productions,
🌐 LampAndLightProductions.com

Donna Paulsen, Soul Hope Ministries,
🌐 SoulHopeMinistries.com

Philip Smith, St. Paul Speaks,
🌐 StPaulSpeaks.com

Tom Meyer, The Bible Memory Man,
🌐 TheBibleMemoryMan.com

Books and Other Publications

Andrew Davis, An Approach to Extended Memorization of Scripture (Ambassador International, 2014)

Tim LaHaye, How To Study the Bible For Yourself (Harvest House, 2006)

Bob Marette, Scriptural Calendar: A Daily Guide To Help You Hide God's Word In Your Heart (Xulon Press, 2012)

The Navigators, Topical Memory System
https://www.navigators.org/resource/topical-memory-system/

R.A. Torrey, The Treasury of Scripture Knowledge (Hendrickson Academic, 1990). Also available online at https://TSK-Online.com. The 1895 edition's title was The Treasury of Scripture Knowledge consisting of Five-Hundred Thousand Scripture References and Parallel Passages from Canne, Browne, Blayney, Scott, and Others.

Notes

Chapter 1 Reality Check: Imagine Life Without Your Bible

[1] Joe Carter, "How Memorization Feeds Your Imagination," The Gospel Coalition, US Edition, Feb. 24, 2015, https://www.thegospelcoalition.org/article/how-memorization-feeds-your-imagination/

[2] Joshua Foer, "Moonwalking with Einstein: The Art and Science of Remembering Everything," (New York: Penguin Group (USA), Inc., 2011), 109.

[3] "Memorize," The Compact Oxford English Dictionary, 2nd Edition, (Oxford: Oxford University Press, 1991), 1062.

[4] Tony Capoccia, "Job 23:3," in Spurgeon's Verse Expositions of the Bible: Job (1999) https://www.studylight.org/commentaries/eng/spe/job-23.html

[5] Robert H. Banks, "Scripture Memorization as a Discipline for Spiritual Formation" (DMin dissertation, Andrews University, 1999) 1, https://digitalcommons.andrews.edu/dmin/503/

[6] According to The Voice of the Martyrs, there are 13 countries where Bibles can be provided by covert means only; another 15 where Bible possession is illegal or highly restricted; and 24 more where obtaining a Bible is dangerous or difficult. See an interactive map at "A Bible for Every Believer," The Voice of the Martyrs, https://www.persecution.com/bibles/ or review the list of nations at "Bibles: Dangerous, Illegal, Covert," Love Packages, https://lovepackages.org/bibles-dangerous-illegal-covert/

[7] "2022 Global Scripture Access," Wycliffe Global Alliance, https://www.wycliffe.net/resources/statistics/

[8] Charles Swindoll, Growing Strong in the Seasons of Life, (Grand Rapids, MI: Zondervan Publishing House, 1983), 61.

Chapter 3 Discover Your Why: Making the Case to Memorize Scripture

[9] J.I. Packer and Carolyn Nystrom, Praying: Finding Our Way Through Duty to Delight (Downers Grove, IL: InterVarsity Press, 2006).

[10] Billy Graham, The Journey (Nashville, TN: W Publishing Group, a division of Thomas Nelson, Inc., 2006), 242.

[11]David Jeremiah, What Are You Afraid Of?: Facing Down Your Fears With Faith (Carol Stream, IL: Tyndale Momentum, 2013), 74.

[12]Life.Church. "How to form a habit – Habits Part 2 – 'Starting' with Pastor Craig Groeschel." YouTube video, Jan. 14, 2019, 30:37. www.youtube.com/watch?v=bXX1kc4xEgQ

[13]Timothy Keller (@timkellernyc), 2014. "When Work Is Your Identity," Twitter, Sept. 12, 2014, 5:25 p.m. https://twitter.com/timkellernyc/status/510539614818680832?lang=en

[14]John Piper, "Why Memorize Scripture," DesiringGod.org, Sept. 5, 2006. https://www.desiringgod.org/articles/why-memorize-scripture

[15]A.W. Tozer cited in Warren Wiersbe, With the Word: A Chapter-by-Chapter Bible Handbook (Nashville, TN: Oliver Nelson Books, 1991), 1507.

[16]John Bunyan, Christian Behavior, ed. George Offor (Chapel Library, 2014), 36-37. https://www.chapellibrary.org/book/cbeh

[17]Victor Garlock, "Garlock: The Benefits of Memorization," The Citizen, Dec. 17, 2019. https://auburnpub.com/lifestyles/garlock-the-benefits-of-memorization/article_a212e6a4-24fe-5e8e-a8f8-cf345904b233.html

[18]Joyce Meyer, "Finding Your Way Out of the Wilderness," ChristianPost.com. https://www.christianpost.com/news/finding-your-way-out-of-the-wilderness.html

Chapter 4 Don't Let the Enemy Fool You: You Can Memorize Scripture

[19]Kazuhisa Shibata, Yuka Sasaki, Ji Won Bang, et al. "Overlearning hyperstabilizes a skill by rapidly making neurochemical processing inhibitory-dominant." Nature Neuroscience 20 (2017), 470–475 . https://doi.org/10.1038/nn.4490

[20]Leslie Basham, "How Busy People Can Memorize Scripture," Revive Our Hearts.com, Jan. 5, 2015: -15:52-15:44.

[21]"How Busy Parents Can Memorize Scripture (with Katherine Pittman), Bible Memory Goal, YouTube video. 16:25-17:19. https://www.youtube.com/watch?v=HYvQaAE3aP8

[22]Denis Waitley, The Psychology of Motivation, (Chicago: Nightingale-Conant, 1993).

[23]For a simple outline of this model, see "VARK Modalities: what do Visual, Aural, Read/write & Kinesthetic really mean?" VARK: A Guide to Learning Preferences, accessed Nov. 21, 2022, https://vark-learn.com/introduction-to-vark/the-vark-modalities/

[24]Kinesthetic learners who use movement to help them focus memorization may also need to repeat that movement to recall the memorized material, so should choose movements appropriately.

Chapter 5 How to Memorize Scripture: The POWER System

[25]As one example, see Adele Ahlberg Calhoun, Spiritual Disciplines Handbook: Practices that Transform Us (IVP Books, 2015), 194.

[26]Telvin Jeffries. "How Working in Short Bursts Could Change Your Life." LinkedIn. May 3, 2021.
https://www.linkedin.com/pulse/how-working-bursts-could-change-your-life-telvin-jeffries/

[27]Joshua Summers, "7 Bible Memory Mistakes I've Made (and How You Can Avoid Them)," YouTube video, 3:56,
https://www.youtube.com/watch?v=No8P3h09W2s

[28]Joshua Summers, "How to Build Scripture Memory Habits (with Pastor Scott Summers)," YouTube video, 0:20.
https://www.youtube.com/watch?v=PvR8KdH7tME

[29]Josh Summers, "How to Use a Memory Palace for Bible Memory (Helpful Tutorial)," YouTube,
https://www.youtube.com/watch?v=t2VH-d8OuSM

[30]Missouri-based MemBands.com offers silicone wristband Scripture memory aids as a way for people to "Tie them [God's words] as symbols on your hands" (Deut. 6:8) to aid the memory process.

[31]Joey Mangelsdorf, "5 Best Bible Memory Apps for 2022 (Memorize the Bible Faster!)," BibleMemoryGoal.com, April 18, 2022, https://www.biblememorygoal.com/memory-methods/best-bible-memory-apps/

[32]The SongsForSaplings.com website provides links to its Spotify, YouTube, Amazon Music, and (Spanish language) Deezer channels, with various sung Scripture and doctrinal content in English, French, Spanish, Ukrainian and Arabic as of this publication.

About the Author

JEREMY KLUTH is the founder of Scripture Alive, a ministry dedicated to engaging people with the Word of Truth to impact real lives. Combining over a decade of acting experience and biblical training from Moody Bible Institute (BA, Communications), he brings the Bible to life through his unique and memorable dramatic Scripture presentations which include whole chapters and stories from fifteen books of the Bible. He also leads Bible Memory Workshops to equip people to memorize Scripture for themselves and does guest preaching to empower people to be fruitful doers of the Word.

Jeremy has ministered nationally and internationally, presenting God's Word live at camps, chapels, conferences, and churches for audiences both large and small, and has traveled to twenty-five countries. God has combined Jeremy's love for Scripture memorization, performance, teaching, ministry, and travel to inspire and instruct people wherever he is invited.

Get more Bible Memory resources at ScriptureAlive.com

Jeremy partners with Healthy Charity and Sandi House

Made in the USA
Monee, IL
13 March 2023

29792586R00090